# more than these bones

# more than these bones

*Bebe Backhouse*

This is a Magabala Book

LEADING PUBLISHER OF ABORIGINAL AND
TORRES STRAIT ISLANDER STORYTELLERS.

CHANGING THE WORLD, ONE STORY AT A TIME.

First published 2023
Magabala Books Aboriginal Corporation
1 Bagot Street, Broome, Western Australia
Website: www.magabala.com
Email: sales@magabala.com

Magabala Books receives financial assistance from the Commonwealth Government through the Australia Council, its arts advisory body. The State of Western Australia has made an investment in this project through the Department of Local Government, Sport and Cultural Industries. Magabala Books would like to acknowledge the support of the Shire of Broome, Western Australia.

Magabala Books is Australia's only independent Aboriginal and Torres Strait Islander publishing house. Magabala Books acknowledges the Traditional Owners of the Country on which we live and work. We recognise the unbroken connection to traditional lands, waters and cultures. Through what we publish, we honour all our Elders, peoples and stories, past, present and future.



Cover Design Jo Hunt
Typeset by Post Pre-press Group
Printed and bound by Griffin Press, South Australia

ISBN (Print) 978-1-922613-65-3
ISBN (ePDF) 978-1-922613-71-4

A catalogue record for this book is available from the National Library of Australia

for anyone whose first love was a painful one.

for those who run with wolves and live bravely as who they are.

for the lovers of the gentle and the kind and the beautiful.

for the people who inspired my words but won't read them.

this is for them.

this is for you.

this is for me.

may we forever dance to the sound of freedom.

and never forget who we are.

# the beginning

LET ME WAKE UP NEXT TO YOU
HAVE COFFEE IN THE MORNING
WALK THRU THE CITY WITH
YOUR HAND IN MINE
AND I'LL BE HAPPY FOR
THE REST OF MY LIFE

## overture

dear you –

i'd like to share with you a little piece of my existence. a small act to introduce myself. to know my now, you need to know my then. certainly, without it and the bruises of its lessons, i have nothing.

my memory tells me this: my father was harsh. my mother was soft. my brother was immature. my sisters were each distant and shielding. so i didn't know my place within the walls of a home and longed for time spent on a pushbike on an open road. a motorcycle on a dry marsh plain. a fort built from old trees in half dead scrub.

i was a popular kid with lots of friends. a second class athlete with first class grades. a born leader. musically talented and a storyteller. in denial of who i was. terrified of the day i'd envelop him. a teenager with bad skin thanks to the genetic lottery. at thirteen my best friend became my first girlfriend, before she sent one of her classmates to break up with me while i waited in line to buy my lunch at the school cafeteria. i was disappointed that this relationship never got given a chance to help me be who i wanted to pretend to be.

at fourteen i connected with my people. by the grandstand on the football field. stolen packets of winfield blue. i'd found my place by losing myself in the beginning of what would be the downward spiral of my teenage years. sweet, sweet alcohol. dirty drugs and cigarettes. random hetero sex. so much of it all. for a young man who was haunted by the childhood i'd had. troubled by the feelings i kept hidden. so resentful to who i saw in the mirror. desperate to change. to be anyone else. anyone.

i know this to be true: i was someone who was born to love. to change the world around me. to make a mark. never wanting to be understood but to understand others. i only wanted to be an enigma to the world, and to me. to make happiness. to find it. and to be exactly whoever the fuck i was destined to be when my life was charted into the stars those billions of years ago. and then some. but the tapestry of my future was scary and i couldn't make sense of it. i went into the world half blind and fully unprepared. with insecurities and fears that were so unrelenting i kept myself awake at night trying to map them out in the dark. as if they were sparklers and fireworks.

i used to wish on shooting stars all the time. they never came true. ever. but i always wished. because i was hopeful. i believed in miracles. the goodness of human beings. i was born into the right world. despite how much i doubted that very thought – of perhaps being too much for this planet and maybe my people were on a different one. regardless, i believed. i hoped. i wished. i moved through the world with kindness. i made friends wherever i went. i had fun. i was wild. i was mostly unhappy. but not sad. and i was free.

on one single night in a hot december, my world changed. it was the beginning of the rest of my life. only i didn't know it. but now i do. and you do too. and so it goes, that i can appreciate my future when it becomes my past. but never the other way around. and i'm glad about that.

it's great to meet you. [you have nice eyes.]

me

## genesis pt i

i remember the night clearly
it tasted of malibu with orange juice
        stained by stale cigarette smoke
        dancing in the humid air to loud music
i was never good at pool
but i tried my best to impress at least one person
with my blue chalk dusting and drunken flukes

i heard them all whisper about the guy in town
a dancer from television
everyone knew        him
everyone wanted        him
no one could have        him

i'd never met        him
yet i knew the stories about
his perfect goatee
his porcelain muscles
his sleeveless shirts

he was untouchable
forbidden fruit
hanging from the highest branch
of the tallest tree
in the furthest place
he was absolutely
incredible
but only
apparently

i butted out my cigarette
took my shot and missed completely
i put down the cue and picked up my glass
and as the straw touched my lips
i heard him laugh

in the corner
in the middle of a crowd
        i saw him
he really *was* captivating
brown skin and dark eyes with a wide smile
begging for heartbeats and attention

he looked at me – he smiled
i looked at him – i smiled back
my desire for him was suppressed
when i ordered another drink
and lit another cigarette

the night went on and i felt him watching me
over the bar and across the floor
        me
the closeted guy who was apparently funny but never confident

i watched him too
over the garden and across the tables
        him
the handsome celebrity who everybody wanted

the bar had closed and i was dragged out the door
i turned my head and he was there
we drove off in our separate taxis in different directions

how could we know
our hearts
would end up
at the same destination?

## genesis pt ii

my cousin had a warm heart
and some would say
too many piercings
she lived in a balinese palace
          open to everyone
          guard dogs on chains
          dancefloor on fire

down the garden path
past the stoners by the pool
i sat at a table
and poured myself a drink

the straw on my lips
i heard a laugh
infectious and annoying

in my avoidance of joints and bongs
i missed him in the middle
keen to escape          him
wanting to know          him

he had somehow come along
to build a home in my head

at the front gate
i met with a friend
passing him in the garden
he was hunched and small
i ignored          him
if only to forget          him

through the grass and palm trees
he was quickly gone
on a shortcut across a bed of flowers
my feet stepped to a stop
the mess where they landed
belonged to          him

i walked upstairs
in search of the bath
and saw him enter a bedroom
to sleep off his alcoholic overdose

        don't follow him
i followed him

opening the bedroom door
i asked him
        are you okay?
rolling in the bed
his loud moan was sure to confirm this

in the instant i closed the door
i was sure
i'd closed our acquaintance but
i didn't know the door was left ajar
a small crack of light
shining into the room

before too long
the door would be thrown wide open
and the light would illuminate
my entire life

## pillow talk [i]

i've always longed for a passionate relationship

no alcoholically fuelled kisses

a wild party's sexual aggression

a divine connection

not just a single night

no casually meaningless fumble

i know life's no fairy tale

but i wish it was less complicated

it'd be so much easier

don't you think?

# diffuser

i'll never stop loving you
i'll always want you
to love me

this is the most amazing feeling in the world
and it's happening

i'm in love
with you

you're in love
with me

and even though nothing else seems right
my entire world is complete

## wonder/lost

we'll always be free
        to move

and we'll always be safe
        to dream

in a sky full of stars
we're two silver comets

we can wander anywhere
        through bustling cities
        or dead grass country

wherever we might go
the world
will always be on our side

wanderlust // made me wonder // got us lost // piha beach AOTEAROA

## scribe

you're my favourite book
the one i'll never tire of reading

when you leave
i place my bookmark in your pages
so i don't lose my place in your story

you've been written by the greatest author
the mind of your own dictation
driven
by the will of your choices

your freedom has given me a rush of adrenaline
the thrill of adventure
softened with romance and trembling fingers

my fingers turn each leaf with an undying need
the anticipation and hunger to know of what will come

your story is
a magical gift which can't be matched
it's for you to live
and me to read

if you ever run out of words
i'll write across your blank pages

and try my best
to honour your splendour

## every day is a lullaby

look at me deeply
        tell me where we're going

speak to me softly
        tell me what we're doing

with all i have
        i'm begging you

don't ever leave me
        you keep my heart alive

## adam

i'll touch your brown skin for as long as my hands can feel

i'll kiss your full lips for as long as my mouth can taste

i'll hold your gentle hand for as long as my arms can move

i'll recite the script of your power if you give me the chance

every line on your face marks each time you've smiled

every crease behind your knees tells the stories you've danced

i surrender into the shape of your strong arms each day

my fingers gently trace the hair trailing across your belly

while you sleep

there's a beauty spot living unseen on the back of your neck

and one silently hiding within the crevice of your navel

there's not enough time to describe the depth of my love for you

i can't put into simple words the meaning of what you are to me

instead

i'll call you beautiful for as long as my voice can speak

and i'll love you for as long as my heart can beat

the first man // impossible // stay where you are // kitekite falls AOTEAROA

## pirouette

we walk

clumsily

around the entire city
we dance drunkenly
through every club

you shuffle over to me
you grab my arms
you swing me around

you twist
i turn

i fall
you laugh

we're a messed-up heap
made of happiness
and heartache

this is
the height of everything we are
this is
the epitome of our love

in our strength and delusion
gently fuelled by addictions
we find nothing can break us
when we're already broken

## pillow talk [ii]

i hear you

when you tell me

you're sorry

you love me

but i need you

to understand me

i don't believe you

i don't forgive you

## smoke

i watch you
through the dark
lighting your rolled cigarette

we're standing in tandem
in a flurry of thoughts

you've been smoking a lot
and i'm starting to question
if you're breathing me in
or blowing me out

## yellow brick road

walk on steadily
don't look back
though the road is dark
you must continue to move
you need to go onwards
further now and further then

you can't stop
i won't let you

keep following my words to the end of this love

## penance // dance in the dark

too many shots
and too many bongs
led me to throwing my guts up into the back garden

i heard the footsteps from around the corner
my head in my hands
and doubled over to kiss the dirt
i could barely see my own feet
let alone those
of the man standing in front of me

he asked if i was alright
i told him i was
he sat beside me
rubbed my back
and i coughed up the last of the tar

he grabbed me
as i stood up
to stumble back to the party
i grabbed him back
just like any other drunk and stoned fool

i stared at him tensely
he stared back with a smile

In

a voice broke the silence
and my body quickly shifted
i turned the corner
and cheered for another drink

although that night saw a huge mistake being made
it saw the realisation
of just how much one person meant to me

if i could go back in time and undo what was done
i would erase the drinks
and the music
and the hurt
and the lies

i would love him harder for knowing he was there
waiting for me
completely present
while i was so unkind

too many shots
and too many bongs
led me to throwing away his trust
for a dance in the dark

## is this happiness?

scream in my face and tell me to hit you
and i'll punch another hole in the wall

look in my eyes and tell me you hate me
and i'll spit at your feet and slam the door

push me over and clench your fist
and i'll pick up a plate and throw it at you

tell me again you think i'm crazy
i don't think i heard you the first time

in case you may have forgotten
i think you're a selfish cunt

i'll walk away now and i won't look back
as long as you search for me

you can't take back the things you've said
but you can tell them to me again next week

you can say you've forgiven the things i've done
but don't ever forget them

we'll throw our hands in the air one more time
we both know this dance by heart

i'll sit in silence and you'll say you're sorry
you'll cry in regret and i'll tell you i love you

eventually we'll stop fighting
then we'll have sex and go to bed

we'll hold each other then turn our backs
and dream of the days when we were happy

## rose garden

my heart is old and aged beyond my own years
and it's not because i've loved too many
but because i've loved too much of you

i can sometimes fall down too easily
and i never call home when i should
and when i'm alone
i slow dance to melodramatic music
without ever really knowing what i want

but i have a memory
of a moment when i looked at you
and sang at the top of my lungs
right before the memory
of when you lost your voice from screaming at me
begins

and i start to wish i hadn't stopped myself from crying
before i could give you the chance to wipe my face

but i don't let myself be brought down by these thoughts
i look at the cobwebs in the corners of the ceiling
i think of the nights in the backyard
when you'd stare at the stars
drinking your whiskey
never a consideration
to tell me why you were quiet and distant

i'd lost myself in our garden
and cowered every night beneath your roses
it was never enough
to live just for this life
if i wasn't living too
for the love i needed

i always remind myself
i need to be careful
to not become addicted to you

i really know
it wouldn't be possible for me to cope
if you were to leave

this

t h i s

is

tough

t h i s

is

love

t h i s

is

not

enough

## morning prayer

in the morning
i said to him

hold on
we're bending

that night
i heard him whisper

let go
this is ending

# the ending

THE ONE YOU LOVE
SHOULD BE THE ONE
YOU DON'T HURT

## a sincere apology

in the silence
we sit completely motionless
my head – heavy on my shoulders
the clock – ticking relentlessly in the kitchen
a reminder that time won't wait for us

we've been fighting and arguing
and we're exhausted
like every time before
my throat is sore
and you're shaking
enough for me to feel the tremor across the room

i can hear you breathe
deep and fast
and in the dull glow of the living room lamp
i see two tears gently roll their way
down both sides of your face

you're still there
in that hazel body
the gentle man i fell fast in love with
the one i could talk to for hours
without direction
i know it's still you who sits in front of me

you still smile the same wide smile
you still laugh the same contagious laugh
you still kiss the same forgiving kiss
your heart just doesn't beat for me anymore

we've reduced each other from boulders to sand
we were solid and honest
but now we sit
absolutely conquered in this certain silence
unable to even look each other in the eye

you know i love you
and i know you love me
and as hard as it is
to not reach out and take your hand
it's too late for either one of us
to even try
and make the smallest of gardens in this mud

i'm so sorry

## a song for january

it was january when we stepped lightly
across the dark red soil
our hands in a tight grip

two brolgas danced in a field by the side of the road
their performance was elegant
moving through the grass with careful choreography
perfectly in sync
with the sound of my heartbeat

pushing through thick brush and trees
we stumbled upon a clearing
overlooking the ocean

we loosened our grip
to breathe in the scent of wattle and salt on the wind
it enveloped our frames
played with our hair
and pushed and pulled us
to the edge of the sea

the sand moved through my toes
and between short strides
my eyes fixed the horizon
i became lost in the sounds of the world
and without stopping
i walked
then began to run
when i couldn't run
i found boats to sail
and when i couldn't sail
i grew wings and flew

in all the amazement and wonder of earth
the colourful reverberations of melodies and songs
there was a silence
louder than anything
and when i looked to my arm
   i saw
   my hand was empty
beside me
   a shadow
   a vacant space
it was once so comfortably full

where did you go?
when did you leave?
the world was ready to be explored with open arms
every mountain
   waiting to be climbed
every river
   crying to be swum
and every forest
   waiting to be walked through
until my bare feet couldn't carry me anymore

i retraced my steps
to all the places i remembered
and as i searched for you
   i found myself
standing still

i'd walked the earth
swum the oceans
flown the skies
          believing
you were right beside me
yet in the still
and the calm
the silence
i remembered
you'd lost your grip
and let go of me

but there was a lust for life
keeping me chasing the wind
and i don't know what happened to you
or in which direction you moved
yet through the cinematic supercut
of memories in my mind
i'll never forget you
your soft hands
and wide eyes
standing in the clearing
among the dandelion
and the thorn

step lightly // dance // to the sound of my heart // the kimberley AUSTRALIA

## delirium kingdom

we were the illustrious princes
of the rundown bars
the self-anointed kings
of the abandoned streets
we were lonely
but we needed no one else
constantly breaking our own inglorious hearts
in search of the next chance
at a better love

we'd forgotten the rules of the night
and knew life never played a fair game
we got drunk in the name of anger
and in the heat of the rage
we'd clench our fists
then waltz to the music of footsteps
in the alleyway outside

devout believers – time is short
convinced – we'd soon be gone
we racked lines – to who we were
we took shots – for where we'd be
making ritual – in memory of the rest of our lives

amid the reality
of the independence we righteously claimed
i couldn't tell you what we stood for
we were young
rebellious against any limit
we thought we knew what we were doing
yet
i can't make any sense of it now

the rights and the wrongs
and everything between
none of it mattered in the middle of a dancefloor
we'd done it before
we'd do it again
          a masquerade through life
          in tragic mistaken pleasure
while never understanding
          we were two men
          who couldn't fly

the passionate kisses
born with a single touch
the earth moving sex
erupting wherever we fell
the nights spent walking home
you on my back
the guiltless moments
lasted forever and never

i'll always remember
our chaotic reign
in the kingdom of love

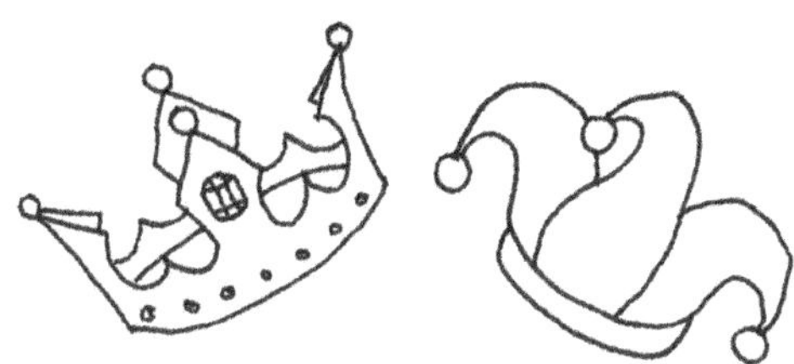

## six a.m.

you'd come home
at six a.m.
scent of black xs
taste of canadian club
dull linger of cigarette smoke
things i knew too well
soaked into your skin
and the clothes you wore

you'd climb into bed
at seven a.m.
scent of dove soap
taste of leftover pizza
crisp sting of listerine mouthwash
the routine i knew too well
laid out before me
a regular demonstration

i'd kiss you
at eight a.m.
scent of ralph lauren
taste of vodka and red bull
fading high of ecstasy pills
things i know didn't belong to you
resting
on your lips and your body

put there by the man
you told me you didn't fuck

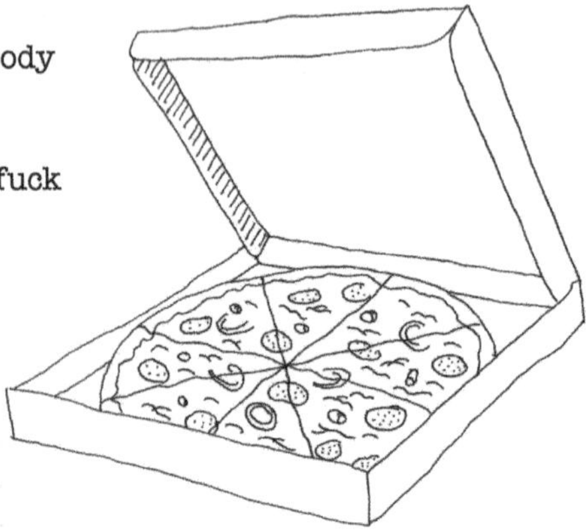

## twenty-one questions

why did you cheat on me? why couldn't you stop?
what was it that made you so unhappy? was it because i lost
control of my weight? had i become
unattractive to you? why couldn't you ever
decide on what it was you wanted?
why didn't you
listen to me
when i
told you that
your drinking
was a
problem?
did you really
think i was a
controlling asshole?
that i was insecure
and jealous?
did you ever think
perhaps your actions made
me that way?
do you remember the
moment you fell out of
love with me?
do you remember the
moment you fell in
love with me?
why were you willing
to throw your home
away for strange men?
do you sit back now
and think it was
all worth it?

where are you now?
do you think of me?
why didn't you fight for me?
why didn't you ask me to stay?
why do i still love you?

## dying by the hand of a man

you came to be so many things to me
but of all the many
you're not a cheater
this isn't a game of monopoly
and you didn't slip paper money under the table

i suppose
i could call you a liar
but i don't feel it'd be harsh enough
maybe
i should call you destructive
but i think i'd seem too sensitive

then i think about the reality of it
i'd freely given you my heart
and despite spent time
the habit of trust
you decided
there wasn't any harm in breaking all of it

you're so much more
than a cheater and destructive liar
you're a murderer
and nothing less than this
because without a thought
you killed something
and you killed it
when it had its back turned to you

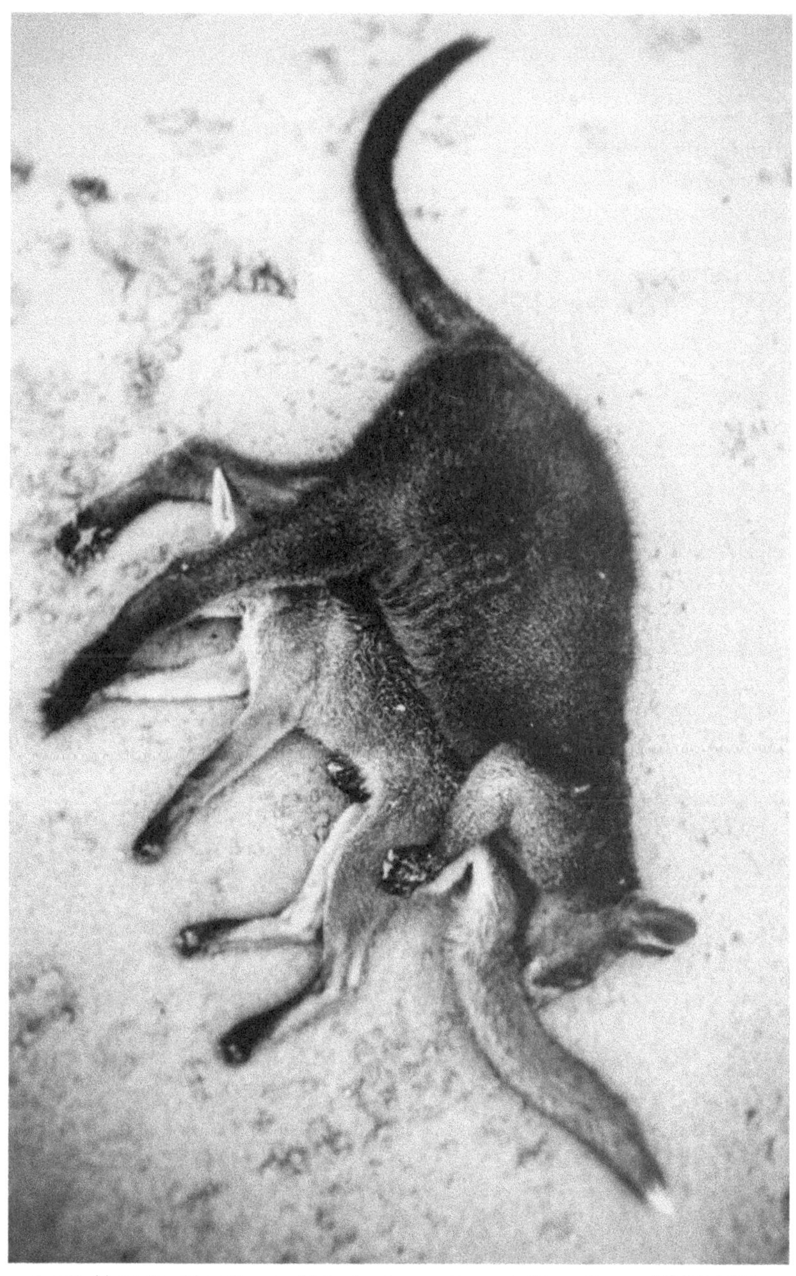

hunt // death // embrace // its back was turned // anglesea AUSTRALIA

## a heartbreak

you were
almost everything to me
you were
the love of my life

you didn't want to be that
and it's such a hard thing to forget

now
i hope
for my own heart
i can somehow
let go of yours

## old friend

you and me
given a chance to start again
rebuild our monument of love
with a different design
dream new dreams
plucked from the clouds they grew within
and grow them
in an irrigated grassland
bordered by briars of real intentions

i cluttered bare walls
with paintings and photographs
which bore resemblance to where we used to be
i placed lamps in corners
on angles which would let me see you
looking your most beautiful
in their dim light

to forgive and not forget – to try again
there was no honour – no pride
only a secret
and a factory of memories
within the cardboard boxes and suitcases you packed

we tried
we failed
you left
i stayed
but we'd tried

a body of concrete and plaster
sat staring vacantly at a lake
beside a river weaving through hills
shards of shattered glass
littered with fragments of broken dreams
an old friend
in the shape of a house
at the bottom of a hill

## open spaces

there's more to this life than you

you're not gravity

or earth

you were the first man to love me

but

you certainly won't be the last

lavender field // open space // beechworth AUSTRALIA

## completely of you

there is comfort to be found here
        in the ebb and flow of my feelings
those which were born
completely of you

in the barrage of your lies
        the constant influx of your dishonesty
i've found one thing
to be hypothetically true
        it's sad
        and it's miserable

but i'm daring myself to believe it
        whether partially
        or completely

I'M FAR BETTER OFF WITHOUT YOU
THAN I EVER WAS WITH

## ponzi scheme

i was in love
and it irritates me so much
to not feel humiliated
or fooled

i'm feeling betrayed
and broken
by a man
i once believed to be
my best friend

## hyde park

in the morning
i think of you
you're not here
but you exist in truthfulness
i find myself alone
in the depth of your freedom

i think of the park bench in paris
and wish you could be with me
because there's no company quite like yours

sit with me

in the night-time
i hear you
your voice hums and lingers
across this city
the cold bites my lips
beneath the graffiti

i think of the ways you held me
and wish you could touch me
because there aren't any hands like yours

make me warm

in my dreams
i remember you
your fabric was detailed
but you were humble
i pursue compassion
beyond this world

i imagine your strength in abandon
and wish you'd love me
because i'd never heard a heartbeat like yours

save me

sit here // think of me // hyde park // london ENGLAND

## dancefloor gore

my heart sat
safely tucked away
beneath my chest plate
large and sheltered
it was strong and brave and knowing
and inside lived love and yen

you tightly clenched your fist
your knuckles strained at the skin
you ripped my heart from its cage
you squeezed it
without letting go

it burst and exploded in your palm
and you were satisfied
so you threw it to the ground

your work here was done
and you wiped yourself clean
on your black jeans

i knelt on the floor
and stared at the mess
plashets of blood
a pile of flesh
tattered and torn into lifeless pieces
colour drained

i collected the remnants of my heart
filled each of them
with freshly cried tears
and i slowly pieced it back together
stitched with delicate threads
of my own sinew

## renaissance // for him

the day you left
was the day i learned to let go
it became
the end of everything i knew about love

i keep on loving
perhaps
a little more careful than before

still
i love

## burning in the distance

we were two different kinds of matter

i was the unwanted ash from a cigarette
breaking at the slightest touch
barely existing
and being quickly forgotten

you were a rock
chipped from a mountain
one which weathers over time
to a pebble
then becomes sand
one day
you'll be dust

you'll be blown with the wind
and you'll travel the world
unfelt and unseen
but you'll surely exist

unlike you
i was too weak
to withstand the pressure
of wind and water

but i was forged in fire
and that's something far greater

light burns in the distance // like me // like you // split point AUSTRALIA

# what becomes of paradise

a thought has arrived
unannounced and uninvited
but it's welcome to sit with me
however long it needs to stay:

after all the time
since we last spoke
and each of my emotional checkpoints
i've expected myself to hate you
for what you've done to me

then it left me
and just as quickly
another had come to be:

– perhaps –
it might be possible to hate you
until you become someone
i could love again

– suddenly –
my heart spoke
rapid and loud:

what i had for you was indeed love
one for who you were
and all you gave
now it is
i can't love you
anymore

## monster

it was always the case
we looked for weakness in each other
when we were hurting
we took it
and we passed it on

i was unhappy
          and i made you miserable

you were damaged
          and you broke me

but i'm free
i hope you are too

## apartment seven

i stare at the blank white walls
remembering
the frames which once occupied the e m p t y s p a c e s

i trace my hands along the furniture
counting creases and scuffs
left by our time

i sit
in dimly lit silence
as footsteps
echo loudly in the hall outside

i sleep in the still
with the windows closed
remembering
who we were
and what used to be

a view // apartment seven // empty space // melbourne AUSTRALIA

## reflection

i could've held onto your sleeve
just a little tighter

i should've tried harder to be honest with you
to be a better person

i wanted to tell you that night
          stay with me – please don't leave

but i've always found comfort in being alone

## i will [not] be happy for you

we haven't spoken in a year
and i don't think we will ever again
but whether it's to be said
or written
i need you to know –

although i wish for you
to be happy and true
i'll never be happy you're with him
you're wonderful
and you're kind
so i'll be happy you're well

## magnitude [an unsent sms]

there's so much i could say to you, but in all honesty there's too much hurt in the way and if we'd meet, what would we gain? most likely a reminder of what we've lost. which would then serve as a reminder itself that you haven't really lost anything. and the question would loom over me –

what exactly was i to you?

i loved you more than you loved me. i was happier with you than you were with me. i was trying to save something you'd already decided you didn't want anymore. and then the tsunami of hurt comes again, where i realise just how much damage you caused.

i'm not angry with you. i'm hurt that you've moved on like i was a 'someone'. when, in reality, you spent one quarter of your life with me. and i shared some of the most significant moments of your life. but like that, i'm treated as if i'm a distant and insignificant piece of your past.

and i never got told the value of the role i played in your life. and i never got told no one will ever compare to me. and i never got told i'll never be forgotten. and the person i was, will always remain with you.

you'll say to people – i loved him once, but we weren't good for each other.

and you'll say to him – i loved him once, but i'm glad i found you.

and all the while, the magnitude of my glow on your life will be forgotten.

I TRIED TO PRESS SEND – BUT I COULDN'T

## pier lane

on the night to end all nights
not a single word was spoken by either of us
it was the kind of silence
which spoke far more
than any word ever could

looking beyond your eyes
to the world within you
my mind whispered to my heart

you'll never look at him the same way

i'll no longer be
the man who runs back to you
every time you push him away
the man you hurt
but who loves you regardless

it was mumbled deep within me

if i was brave
and if i was honest
i'd tell you this –
i accept you for who you are
just as i'd accepted
everything you once gave to me
and everything you took away again

i'd say it so loud
and so clear
then you'd know it
and i'd know it
and i could never take it back

but i wasn't brave
and i wasn't honest
and all we did was look at each other
already knowing
what was needing to be said

on the night to end all nights
when not a single word was spoken
by either of us
in the silence
which spoke more than any word could
i was the first one to look away

pier lane marina // not a single word was spoken // melbourne AUSTRALIA

## if i'm being honest

i know i've made a lot of promises over the years
promises i had every intention of keeping
but when it came to the moment of being true
i didn't have the strength
or commitment
to follow through
and deliver on my word

i promised
i'd stop hurting myself
after you'd found my bloodstains in the bathroom sink
you never understood why they were there
but i made sure
you never saw those stains again
because i learned to be more careful at cleaning them

i promised
i'd never be unfaithful to you again
the thought of crushing your swollen heart
one more time
made my stomach tighten
and although i never did give my body
to anyone else again
i made sure to delete the text messages
before you could find them

i've made so many promises over the years
i've lied to your face
and fucked with your head
i know words are meaningless
without foundation
but there's one promise i made
i know i'll keep

i promised
as long as i live
i'll never forget who you are

petit à petit

a velvet night
by a crimson day
you left me

a virile man
by an obscure bedroom
you betrayed me

the desperate fight
by the hopeless grasp
you damaged me

in the seldom moment i cross your mind
you'll know –

the certain day
by the ensuing night
i stopped looking for you

a gentle memory
by a partial belief
i began to forget you

little by little
and just a little more
i stopped loving you

## reverie

i open my eyes and the house is quiet and empty
i turn on the kettle and make myself a coffee
a day like today is a day when i want you
i want you to share your air with me
i need you to be nowhere but here with me
and in the silence i hear your key turn in the door

it's so nice to see you

your nine a.m. end of weekend routine begins
        you eat
        you shower
        you call me to bed

the moments of me wanting your air
and needing you to be with me become real
then with every touch and every kiss
the cold air vanishes
and we sweat until we're one

the anger i felt for you
for leaving me
so you can chase drunken bliss
and the loneliness which crept up on me
when you'd pursue your bent highs

        they're gone

the air regains its bite
you re-dress to find comfort
and you fall asleep within seconds
your gentle snoring breaking the silence

i'm not tired though
i've got things to do

but you're soft
you're warm
you're addictive

and it's so nice to see you

today is a day when i want you
i want you to share your air with me
i need you to be nowhere but here with me
so
i stay in bed with you for a few more minutes
i put my arm over you
you're soft and you're warm and i fall asleep within seconds

i open my eyes and the house is quiet and empty
i turn on the kettle and make myself a coffee

## adieu

to your masculine torso
	passing through corridors and doorways
the breaths left behind
	to hang in the air
i say goodbye

your enigmatic eyes
	bearing no depth or end
	a force consuming everything i have
i bid them farewell

to our love
this love we gave
	and took
without question
a song played softly
	out of time
	out of tune
so long

you're gone
	my love
so long!

## sail on

you were a ship in the night
destined by fate
to spend the course of your life
sailing through the oceans
on an endless journey

one stormy night
you arrived on my shores
in search of shelter
you stayed longer than you or i had ever expected
and i thought my island
was where you'd make your home
where you'd see each storm through
from the safety of my forest

as life would have it
you were just visiting
and a cold wind
saw you once again set sail
in search of a new and unfamiliar land to explore
leaving me motionless
tied to the ocean floor
as islands stay

gazing the horizon
hoping a strong breeze
might throw you off course
and i'd see your billowing sails
and your tall mast
returning in my direction

just as your footprints will remain etched on me forever
my sand and trees and waterfalls
will always be yours
this special place
even if you never set foot on my beaches again

and if the wind will blow
then let it blow now
and i'll either wait for you
or forget you

dear lover // your mast was tall // sail on // williamstown AUSTRALIA

## chapel street

you and i
we always knew
what we had was special
but just like everyone else
we had our ups and downs

you and i
we'd always hoped
to work through the bullshit of life
continuing the intense
but simple devotion
we'd always shared

you and i
we decided to go our separate ways
we're passionate
stubborn and ambitious
you and i
we really do love each other
but we're just like everyone else

## a memory of dust

the porch didn't feel the same that night
when i stood in its centre
and watched you walk toward me

i'd never seen your eyes
so dark with fear
yet you were far braver
than you'd ever realise

what we'd known
for so long a time
we avoided like the plague
but it still consumed us

you accepted it
as fate bestowed on us
and you pinned it proudly
to your shirt

it was a badge
to forever remind you of what you had
and what you chose to leave behind
to save yourself – us

i held my breath
as you placed your hand on my shoulder
as you pulled me into your chest

i could feel what rested
beyond your heartbeat
in between the rise and fall
of your ribcage

i knew you were lost to me forever
and in the moment of turning my back

i uttered a goodbye
and you turned to dust

## flinders street station

do you know what i miss the most today?
i miss the fights we'd have

you'd tell me
you thought our fights meant –

we didn't love each other
as much as we used to

we were falling further away
from what we were
and into something
you didn't want to be

when i close my eyes
and see the two of us standing there
fighting and shaking
exhausted

i see two people
scratching their heads
asking –

how can i love you better?

## you have been loved

i loved all your moments
i received your neglect and your grace
i saw the beauty within your heart

whether it was true or not

i felt
the spirit of your changing face

i admired
the freedom of your gypsy soul
the temporary home it found in me
how you only ever moved to the beat of your own drum

## love young love

love
my young love
you're the only one
who came to know me so well

even now
our story might be over
it will always be
my favourite one to tell

# the others

DO WE HELP PEOPLE
COS WE SEE THEM AS GOOD
AND WE WANT THEM TO SHINE
IN THEIR GOODNESS?
OR DO WE HELP THEM
COS WE WANT TO SHARE
IN THEIR GLORY?

## germany

it was your vulnerability
and your sadness
your quiet desperation in needing someone
that drew me close to you

you had a huge heart
a deep soul i could've gotten lost in
but i didn't get lost
i didn't love you
as you thought i did
and i certainly didn't need you

it hurt when i looked at you
you were completely unaware
when your eyes lit up
and you'd smile at me
i was counting down the seconds
till i could leave

you were a distraction
keeping me occupied
you filled my cup when it was empty
and i knew
you'd never be anything more

you kept me warm
you made me feel wanted
you appreciated the things i didn't – i couldn't
you challenged the way i looked at the world

if i wasn't selfish
if i was able to let go of my pride
if i'd allowed my stubbornness to fall away
you'd have been a kind of perfect for me

but it was your vulnerability
and your sadness
your quiet desperation in needing someone
that pushed me away from you

## amsterdam

bebe!
listen to me:

why would you stay with someone who treats you this way?
you deserve so much more than what you're given
there's nothing wrong with you
don't blame yourself
if this were a different life – i'd sweep you off your feet

the stranger i knew
as an englishman in a dutch bar
was convincing me there was such a thing
as a man who's kind and generous
and warm and loving
he was reminding me
of my value and my worth

before i could speak
we'd kissed
his lips were soft
his breath was warm
he kissed me with ferocity and strength
showing me the feeling
i'd forgotten before

and in that moment
i came to know
    what i didn't have
    what i wanted
    what i deserved

and forever from then
i burned his eyes into mine
i memorised the last words he spoke to me
before he turned and left

promise you'll never forget yourself
you'll get what you deserve
you'll never settle for less

i made the promise
to a human i'd never known
and kissed just once
and with my man beside me
i wandered across amsterdam
drinking and drifting
into the early morning light

all the while
with every corner we turned
every cobblestone street we walked
every bridge we crossed
and every club we danced
i searched
for the englishman i met in the dutch bar

unable to find him
unable to forget him

the streets called to me // i searched for him // amsterdam NETHERLANDS

## awake

in my room
there was no light
except the glowing beacon outside the window
i was alone in bed
lying in thoughtless existence

slowly
the door opened
and your silhouette
hovered in the frame

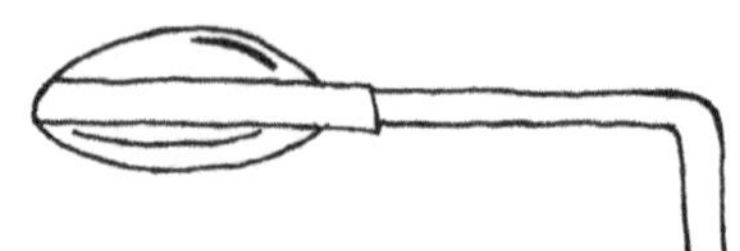

i stared
without saying a word
as you moved to my side

my eyes were locked on yours
as yours were on mine
the moment
could've lasted for hours
but i think it was only a few seconds

then you leaned down
and our lips met
and for the first time
my mind relaxed

my body took over
i closed my eyes
and it was then i woke up
alone

i told myself to sleep it off
tomorrow
i'll have forgotten all about you

yet here i am
all these years later
still trying
to sleep you off

# flamingo

on a dark and stormy night
you were the blazing fire
which warmed me from the inside
when i was wet from the rain
and stained with mud
you took off my clothing
carried me down the hallway
into the bath to wash me
and when i'd fallen asleep with my head in your lap
you gently pressed my cheek
and told me i was beautiful

i could've sat forever
watching your eyes move as you'd tell me
about the simple intricacies of your day
my hand in yours

you were delicately romantic
forcefully passionate
time failed to exist when you kissed me
on the kitchen bench
the living room floor
the front seat of your car

what a rush it was
        to be swiftly swept off my feet
        to dance across a marble floor with you
        under the celestial eyes of iridescent stars

what a short and beautiful time we had
and if time proved anything
it was
for a moment
i might've been yours
but you could never be mine

## you pt i

keep me perched on the edge of your darkness
i don't want you to illuminate me at all
i just want to sit
and watch your rainbow
as you dance across heaven in peregrine motion
your movement
and your emotion
remind me of an eruption of stratocumulus clouds
falling from the open sky

i watch you – i want you
i can see you – i can feel you
your electricity
and desire
and fire
your magnetism

your hands lift me up to dance with you
like a tree growing from the earth
into the field of light
beneath the stars
spring is finally here
and it's guiding me to feel the petals on your skin
your pollen caresses my skin and kisses my face

this is pure nature
in the rush hour of our commute
through time and space and all its dimensions
i want to see you more than i want to feel you
you're giving me life
and depriving me of nothing
you're adrenaline
you're life's greatest mystery

the unanswered questions of our origins
lie in the abyss of your eyes
i can have faith i'll be welcomed into your paradise
in you – i find the hope of everlasting life
i summon an angel to keep me in the dark
over and over again
it's you
tall and light

you're energy and gravity
a life force
concepts remaining unknown and unseen
love and life

my emotions don't have a face
but they do have a name
the name is strong
and it's made from light
the name
is yours

## pyrite

don't get ahead of yourself and think for one minute
          i want to be with you
          i've been desperately longing for you

i haven't spent the last decade
dreaming of you

you can't be the one who got away
because
i was the one who ran

## moses

i'll always remember
the time i spent waiting for you

i'd given you a piece of me
and it might not have been the biggest bit of my heart
but
it was all i could offer you

thank you
for choosing me
to be the one you held on to for a moment in time

i knew we'd meet our end
and in the measure
of minutes and hours
it wouldn't seem like long

but in the concept of parallel time
through the cosmos
and the universe

it could've lasted
forever

## anthony

my dear old lover
i found myself thinking of you tonight

this time was different from every other
because i didn't just think of your stubbled face
or your firm body
and powerful hands

i thought of your spirit
and everything it ever represented
all those years ago
and still now

i owe you more than what i ever gave
more than what i ever knew
what i refused to acknowledge

do you think
if i spoke to you more sweetly
more honestly
you might have stayed?

i like to believe you would've followed me
        thrown on a jacket
        jumped in your car
        dogs on the back seat

driving through the night until it was day
over
and over
and over again
until we met in the doorway of my house

i suppose
in hindsight
there's a bitter sweetness
which comes late at night
creeping in with a gentle draught

i realise things could be different
perhaps a better different
to what is now
where we didn't say goodbye

but it's in the realising
i peacefully remember
          who you were then
          who you are now
and it's enough to send me gently to sleep

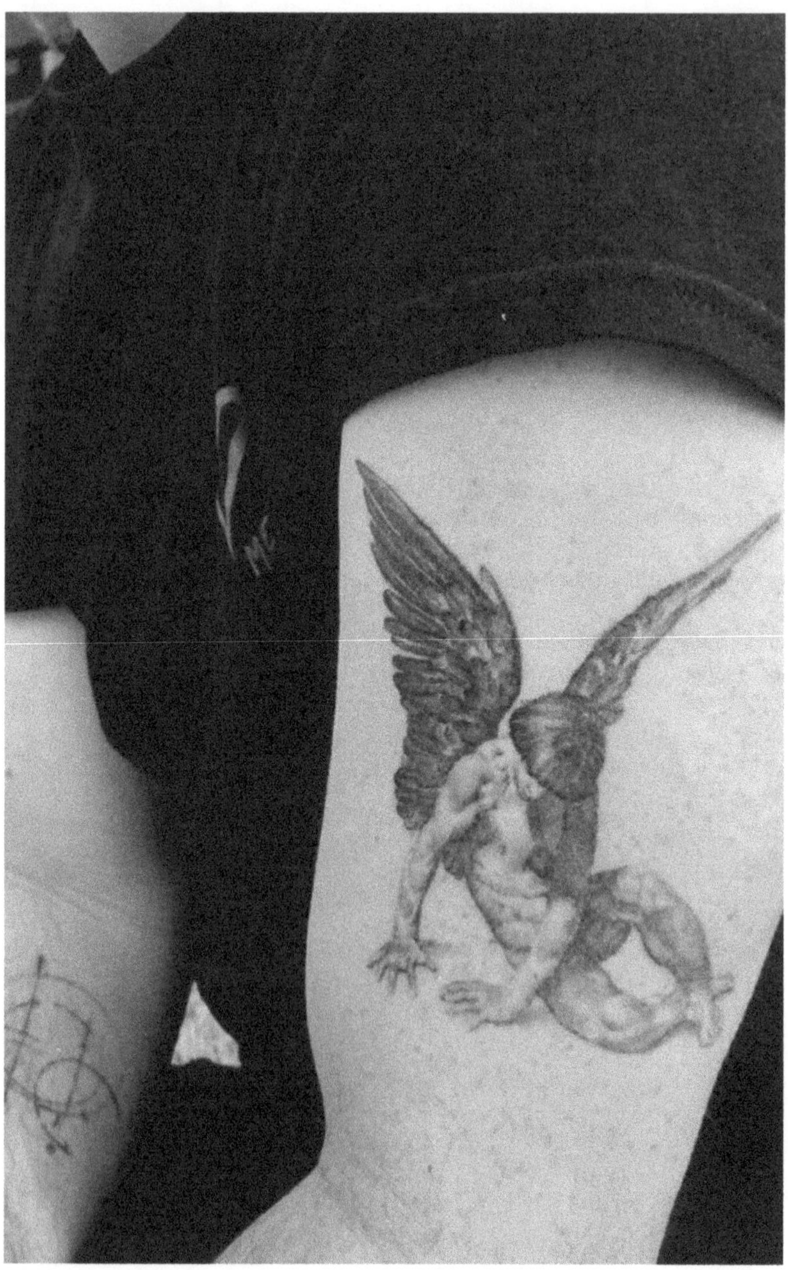

anthony // and his tattoos // he believed in angels // brunswick AUSTRALIA

i thought i found the man
i'd always been waiting for

but i found myself
trying to turn him into someone new

someone
he was nothing like

the someone
was you

## the things you fear

we were two people who loved each other
whether we'd done this perfectly or not
we'd tried tirelessly to live life together
whether perfectly or not
we'd lived each day by the other's side
and we traced the deepening lines
which had formed
across the other's face

we were two people who had one dream together
and we allowed the one dream
to slowly
but surely
be replaced
with two separate and less positive
less determined
less significant dreams

we were two people
on two separate journeys

i sat in silence
as the night grew deeper and darker
all through the next day
as it stretched
into the next night
as it returned
and i realised –

one of us
had loved the other ferociously
and the other hadn't

one of us
had watched the other carefully
and the other hadn't

one of us
had listened intently
and the other hadn't

one of us
had remembered the dream
and held onto the meaning of that one dream
for much longer
than what the other thought was reasonable
whereas the other one of us
perhaps walking down a silent street
had carelessly thrown it away

i'm hurting
but i'm breathing

i'm aching
but i'm alive

i love you
but i'll go on without you

## you pt ii

you're the footsteps coming from down the hall
the anticipation building within me
the ocean which churns in the depth of my deepest cavity
you rise in ecstasy
as i collapse in spent composure
your breath breaks my fall
and we're surrounded by vibrations
your frequency rises when the sun goes down
your colours guide me
like butterflies

touch me
and lead my face to your night
where you live as hope in infancy
like an embryo in the womb
i swim through murky water
to find peace with you there
before this life ages us too far

your moods are as ambiguous
as the darkness concealing me
your blood is my blood
and it courses through my veins
like a crimson tide on a blank canvas
if your rivers ever run dry
then most surely i'll die

you're my eyes wide shut
shielded in leather
i beg for your fingers around my throat
your fire blazes down my neck
your kisses envelop my back
sealed by our perspiration and elation
over and over again
i am you
and you are me

you represent the very length of this poem
and these words
which are mine
keep flowing out of my soul
it's a rapturous abandon
surrendering to the oxygen
then breaking against the riverbanks
trembling with pleasure
unable to stop
like a w
a
t
e
r
f
a
l
l
and climaxing against the firm flesh of the earth

you're pink and blue
yellow and orange
you're a fire
a silhouette against an open window
making love to the sunrise
you're ecstasy and energy
you are
the entire universe

## leonardo

i could mould you into the man
i want you to be

but i know that man
would never be happy
or free

SACRIFICING YOUR HAPPINESS
FOR THE HAPPINESS OF SOMEONE YOU LOVE
TO KEEP SOMETHING
PRECIOUS TO YOU
IS BY FAR THE TRUEST TYPE
OF LOVE

## the night

i could tell you
i won't hurt you again
but it's safer
for me to let you go

## l'amour sans paroles

les mots que j'ai écris
ont suivis leur but
cependant
ce sont les mots que je n'ai pas écris
qui continuent de me hanter

donc
je me demande
si l'amour que tu m'as donné
est suffisant pour servir ton but
ou es tu hanté
par ce que tu as gardé?

--

the words i wrote
have served their purpose
yet
it's the words i didn't write
which continue to haunt me

so
i wonder then
of the love you handed me
if you gave enough to serve your purpose
or are you haunted
by what you kept?

## eros

my dear lover
i'm the servant of your affection
i sit by your side
and stare upon your naked body

your skin glows
as it dances
against the flickering wicks of the candles
your eyes are closed
with your head tilted backward
your spine – arched so tensely

your hips move up and down
and you pant
as the orgasmic waves ebb and flow
throughout your entire existence

you shake
you scream
as the pleasure showers over every cell within your body

my dear lover
how can i not serve you?
how can i be so selfish and rob you of such ecstasy?
how can i be so ignorant and deprive myself of such joy?

i know who i am
i've been searching
but now i know my truth
i'm the servant of your affection

and you?

you're my pathos
my cupid
my eros
the meaning of love

## benediction

i won't say goodbye
no – my love
i'll thank you

you came to me
you gifted me happiness
you loved me
you let me love you in return
you gave me so many memories to cherish

maybe the most of all
you've shown me
soon there'll come a time
when i'll let you go

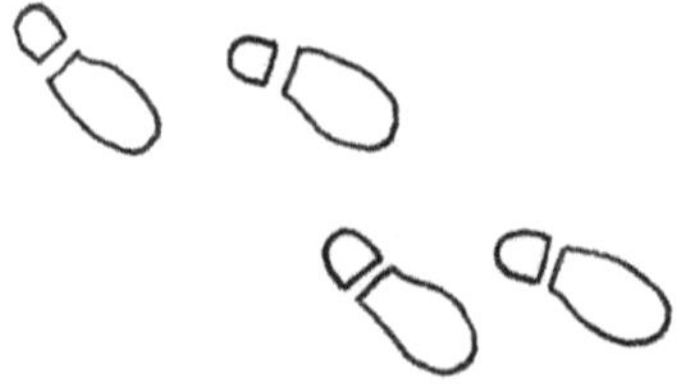

## bedside table

i could love you desperately
and pray
your heart will only beat for mine
but as embers die to soot and ash
so has my love and my patience
i won't wait for you anymore

keep me now on your bedside table
not in the dusty drawer
you don't need to look at me every night
just give me the chance
to watch you while you sleep

## francis

if i imagine the world without you
there'd be only darkness

the ocean of stars
        stretching boldly across the sky
        as we dance beneath it
gone

the sun
        turning your hair
        from vanilla brown to golden yellow
        and your eyes from blue to green
disappears

the magnificent moon
        all its shapes we've come to know
        from laying side by side
        on the bonnet of your car
        your hand in mine
vanishes

in this darkness
there's no way
to softly trace your face
there's no love
no kindness
no hope

if i imagine the world without you
then i see only
the end

## flowers in northcote

the sun hits my eyes in a sudden flash
you
in your khaki jacket
clinging tightly to your phone
your beanie wrapped around your head
hiding your hairline from me

i could think about whose name you might be reading
what text you might be typing
or if the photos you took of yourself this morning
were for me
or for someone else

but i won't waste time
thinking of all the things that could be
i won't question the reason you're quiet today
because
when we're trying to remember where we parked the car
and you hold my hand

i feel warm again
just like the sunlight
that blinded you when you shifted your gaze
from the barista inside
to the man across the street
then to the vibrating iphone in your hand

how in that quick moment
you missed the smile i gave you
because the sun captured you perfectly

and you didn't see the bird landing beneath your chair
to eat the crumbs of your croissant

and you didn't hear the car driving by
playing your favourite song with the windows down

i stood on the footpath
and waited for you to pay the bill
i saw a man walking with flowers
and i thought for a short while
what it'd be like
if you gave me yellow tulips
instead of silence

there was coffee // but no flowers // northcote AUSTRALIA

## when the sky is dark

i'll pick you up later
when the sky is dark
when there are fewer people on the streets
and less thoughts on your mind
i prefer to know you when she's not around
you always seem happier
when you're alone

i drive 120 straight down the m80
along the western ring
past essendon fields
and i weave through traffic
pretending my car and the lines
are my fingers in your hair

oil stains and asphalt
pine trees and eucalyptus
the suburbs change
as the skyline fades
from my place to yours

there's no difference between us
except for the lies we tell
our timing is everything
and this time is no different

the only reality we'll ever need
is the measuring cup
filled with the nights we spend together
not those we don't

the headlights from the cars
flicker
between yellow and orange
then crystal and blue
like the flowers you sent me on my birthday
still sitting in my kitchen
pressed between books
out of sight from anyone who sits at my table

i'll pick you up later
when the roads are empty
we can go to the drive-through cinema
or the park by the creek
but only meet me when the suburbs are quiet
and the sky is dark
close to midnight
when she's asleep

## patience

the path i walk
is destined by my fate
no matter where i step
destiny doesn't recognise reality
there in the footfall

so on and forward
i'll walk
till i can find a seat
and removing my shoes
sit there quietly

comfortable
in casual sunday clothing
all the while
waiting patiently to see you

# the bones

CAN KILOMETRES REALLY SEPARATE YOU
FROM SOMEONE ELSE
WHEN IF YOU'RE WITH SOMEONE YOU LOVE
AREN'T YOU ALREADY THERE?

## grief is a terrible dinner guest

losing her was a strange thing
grief broke me
left me incapacitated
the belief there was no future
only a past
capturing empty dinner plates
and cups stained with water marks

no more late-night talks
over winfield and moccona
questioning who my new boyfriend might be
now the former had left me

no more drives
down linlithgow and victoria
diamond rings clutching
a black handbag and oversized sunglasses
picking dripped chocolate
from knee-length pants

one night
i fell asleep
and while i dreamed
grief decided it didn't want to stay any longer
clear vision blurred
like a fogged windscreen through rain
no day the same again
just broken thoughts
reflected on roads in oil stains

the mantra on russell
tram stop 10 on swanston
just memories that appear to be fragments
of someone else's life i read about once
on a bench in thornbury park

the last time // the bench in thornbury park // ascot vale AUSTRALIA

## little one

i never understood what you were feeling
or what it was you were going through

i think i was afraid of understanding
because i didn't want to admit
i didn't know best

if i'd tried to see through your eyes
then i could've helped you
and you might be okay

my god. despite all the good things, i'm not really happy.
i'm still hurting from everything that's happened.

we separated a year ago last week and i still can't bring myself to move on from him. i can't do it, yet he's moved on so easily.

which only goes to show he'd already let go, when we were
still together and i was still holding on.

i think about my nan all the time, and things with her are
just so blurry. my memories are changing bit by bit, and i don't feel the impact of her being gone like i used to.

i'm not happy in this house. i love my home, but i don't want to live like this anymore.

i know my break will come. the journey will be long and hard, but worth it in the end.

i know this, but i don't have the patience for it. i wish i could go back in time and do so many things differently.

i'd hope things would turn out somehow otherwise today.
it's just not possible and now i have to keep moving forward
every day.

like i have been. and i know i can do it.

i'm just not happy like i used to be. but you already knew
this.

## baobab

i will never deny
you know me
better than any other
and despite the vast distance between us
we will always be close

even on dark days // you still love me the most // derby AUSTRALIA

## craindre

i was never afraid of you dying
i was never afraid of you leaving

i was afraid
of looking into your eyes
and for the first and last time

saying goodbye

## only fools

please
don't look at me like that
you know this isn't me
look beyond what you see
to the person you know me to be

this is hard for you
i know you're scared of losing me
you think every time you see me
might be the last

trouble has always managed to find me
i've tried running away
but i've got big feet
and i always trip on them
and it's you
who's always there to catch me

i hope you believe me
when i tell you
i'm sorry

for letting you down

embarrassing you

not being the man
you hoped i'd become

please
don't turn away from me
i'll stand on my own
i'll find my way in this world
i'll make you proud of me

i just need you to help me

## elegy for a rose

i was lying in bed with her one night
and while i waited for her to drift off to sleep
we started talking

we had our usual conversations
stories of when she was younger
her prolific career
the hilarious comments she'd make about people

then she turned to me
and with determination in her face she said
    i don't want to die
    i'm not ready
    i'll fight this

i looked at her
and thought for a moment
completely unsure of what to say

she
was a woman
who always knew what she wanted
and she always got it

she wasn't afraid of anything
never backed down from a hard situation
and when things got tough – you know how it goes

yet
there she was
the strongest
most fierce woman i knew
in her black and white striped pyjamas
exposing her soul to me
as scared and fearful

after a short while
i brushed my fingers through her hair
and said

    no one's ever ready to die
    and for what it's worth
    i don't want you to die either
    you're right
    you'll fight this

i knew
her polluted body
wouldn't recover
i also knew
she'd fight
with every ounce of strength
in her saltwater blood
and she did

as the weeks went on
even on her weakest days
when she had no energy to stand
she'd still do
what she needed to do

she'd make me mad
she'd make me laugh
she'd request her cup of dilmah tea
eight times a day

she was so strong
she was so courageous
i wanted to beg her to stay
but i knew she wouldn't
she couldn't

with my mum beside me
i laid in bed with her
just like i'd done
so many times before
and i held her tightly
as she took her last breath

now
for me
her life and her presence
are frozen in time

she was charismatic // magnetic // electric
and everybody knew it

she was such a unique hybrid of a woman
whenever she walked into a room
everyone stood up to talk to her

to many
she was known as chief // madame chair

to me
she'll always be my magnificent nan
my beautiful rose
and i'll always be her golden child

it was our one-of-a-kind bond
that allowed me to truly understand her
and love her completely

i loved her
i loved her – i loved her
i still love her – i always will

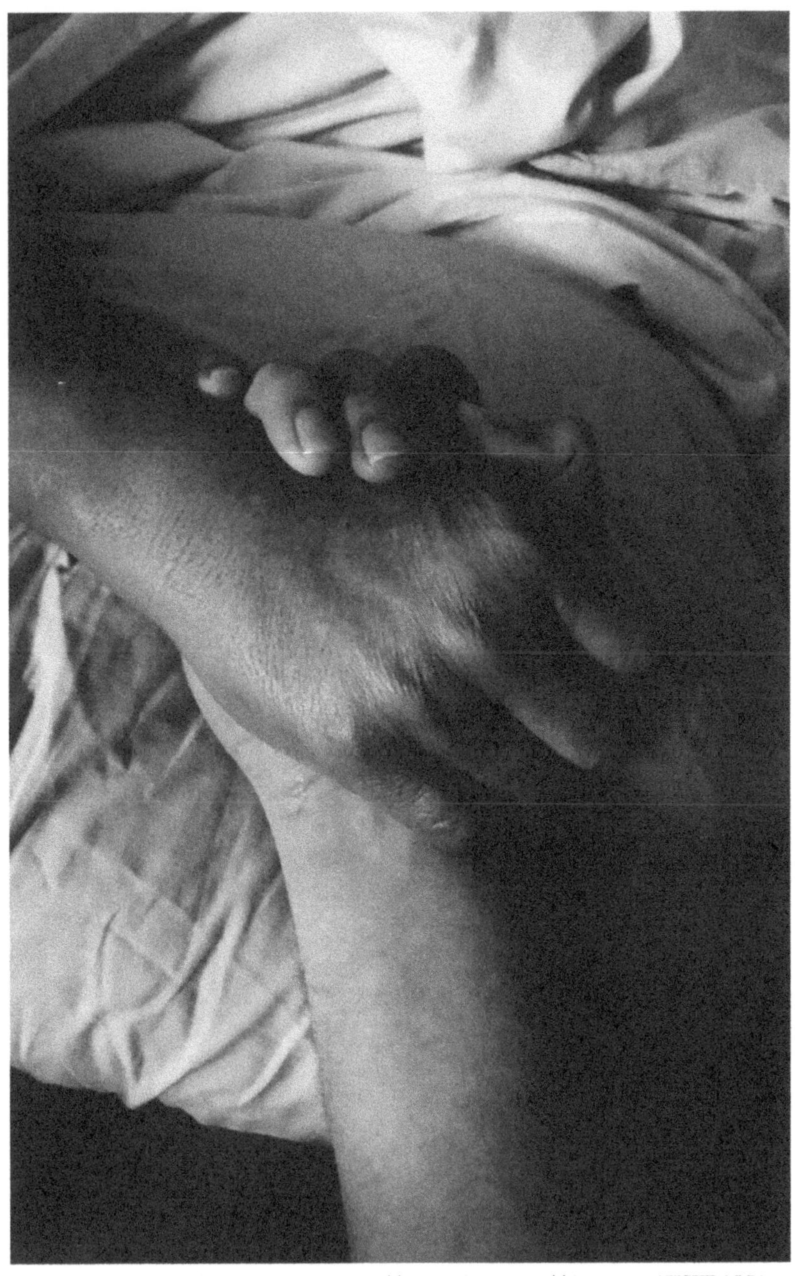

grief found me // the day she died // i won't let go // broome AUSTRALIA

## testimony to a wilted flower

my blood nose drips
as my eyes glow red
my bare feet
hit chipped pavement

cracked lips
mumbling dignity

the streets are filled
with blurred-out faces
and broken bottles litter the roads
like diamonds
burned out foils crumple and fall

stale smoke
cloudy judgement

my room is dark and cold
drunken men carelessly stagger
in and out
my heart is weak
i'm lonely

this silence
echoing absolution

## decay

i feel i didn't lose you at once
instead
with each day that passes
it's like i forget some other part of you

yesterday
i tried to remember the sweetness of your perfume
but it didn't smell the same

today
i tried to recount the rings on your hands
but the fingers changed
each time i did

tomorrow
i'll think of the last drive we took through my suburb
but i know the streets will seem shorter
than they really are

i wish in part
i'd lost you at once
yet i find myself
losing you
day by day
piece by piece

## the bardwell house

she sat in the living room
with one leg folded behind the other
sipping carelessly
on her cup of milky tea

one sat at the dining room table
trying to complete the final crossword in the book
the other
cleaning to be distracted
from the silence of the house

she stared
out into the backyard
through the patio
and watched the man by the fence
she was sure
she'd seen him before
he was peculiarly familiar
as if she knew him once

his face
right then
was so different to what it once was
there were so many questions to be asked
about the strange man at the fence
but no question
was asked out loud
and no second thought was given to him
once he disappeared
from her imagination

he'd existed once
as much as she was alive then
but she closed her eyes
and fell asleep
as her cup of tea sat cold
the house not clean
the crossword unfinished

she closed her eyes // the walls keep secrets // broome AUSTRALIA

## the apple and the tree

as i am me
and it's no one's place
to tell me not to be
what i am

my father is my father
and it's not my duty
to tell him to not be
that which he is

things are really hard for me at the moment. i feel weak, and i'm not sure i can get through this.

you left me not long ago, and i thought that's where the pain was meant to end. the phase where i try to fill the void you left behind would begin.

where the happy memories, positive thoughts, and warm rays of sun on my face – all these things – emphasised by the thought of you –

would allow me to begin to feel content. and i'd be able to heal from the wound of having to say goodbye.

nothing seems to be getting any better. my spirit doesn't appear to be lifting.

i'm back in the familiar comfort of my house, yet i feel like i'm in a strange place. you always told me i lived too far away, and i needed to come back and be closer to home.

and for the first time, i think i actually agree with you.

in all this heartache and sadness, i know that i'll get better. i just wish, with everything i have, i could tell you how i feel.

not to hear you respond, but to be satisfied that i've spoken to you. and i could rest easily, knowing i'd heard your voice again.

because when you were here –

i was okay.

CALLED HER PHONE // KNEW SHE WOULDN'T ANSWER
LEFT A MESSAGE // TO FEEL LESS ALONE

## blue china bowl

how many beginnings

are held at bay

because

we refuse to allow

an ending to be an ending

it's not perfect // it holds things // safely inside // kensington AUSTRALIA

## purgatory

the ceiling is resting on my forehead
there's another dimension
between me and the world outside
my heart beats fast
through the layers of clothing
pushing my blood through the veins of my neck
        into my ears
        out to the walls of my room

beyond the door
lana del rey sings to me
she was an angel
in the land of gods and monsters
must be where i am now
        purgatory
between the earth and the sky
too afraid of heights to go higher
too anxious at the idea of going backward
to think about turning around
so choosing – to stay still

i used to judge the people
however unfairly or righteously
the random cars
arriving at the houses we're familiar with
how they'd step into the light
        or the dark
refusing to break eye contact with the ground
as they scratched their arms
sniffing hard and fast
hands outstretched
a desperate tremble

they were the people we avoided
not out of fear of unwelcome conversation
but out of disgust
        they were beneath us
their dirty fingernails and matted unkempt hair
their ripped clothes
clinging to their bones
like static energy

but who am i to speak
on where i stand in society – compared to them?
when now –
there's a shared algorithm
that counts me with the association to trouble

the smoke enveloped them
like it's done me
and we all scramble relentlessly
        like ants
in an organised chaos
desperately searching

searching for a sweetness better than honey
a breath of life more compelling than oxygen
an intense thirst water won't quench

we stare through windows
to the world outside
where kids are riding bikes on dusty footpaths
and lovers are kissing over cocktails on beaches
while we fearfully frivol through this space
between the earth and the sky

## birdsong

the birds are calling
the grass is softly rustling

every sound of the wild
which shows life is still being lived
harmonises
with the voices of our people

it's a dreamtime song
and they're singing
for you

sat below a tree // a bird called // we sang together // parkville AUSTRALIA

WE DON'T BAND TOGETHER
WE PIT ONE AGAINST THE OTHER
EACH OTHER
FOR THE TITLE OF THE BEST
BUT THIS BEHAVIOUR IS THE WORST

## wherever you are

days turned to weeks
and those weeks to months
the months have come
and they've passed on by

i still think of you
each and every day
i sleep with your book
sat in a drawer beside my bed

your smile
your laugh
only imaginary in my mind
and sometimes
i think i can see you
and i pretend you talk to me

i can't ever hear what you say
but i always know what you mean

i try
again and again
to send you my message
wherever you are
and in what time
i know it'll reach you:

i miss you incredibly

and i love you even more

## crochet blanket

i still remember the feeling
of laying with you
as you took your last breath

and i'll never forget the lifetime of stories
passing between your shoulder and my head
leaving me
wanting more

the memory of your soft skin has stayed with me
as the only warm blanket i'll ever need

## lullaby

soft little love

lift up your head

don't give up now

your dream isn't dead!

## twelve // april

my first birthday
spent with my family in seven years
my first birthday without her

every year without fail
on the twelfth of april
she'd call me to ask if it was my birthday
even though she knew it was
and every year without fail
the same grateful conversation would be spoken

although i knew it wouldn't come
i still waited for the phone call
to complete the anniversary of my arrival

going forward
life will never be the same
her presence can still be felt
but her voice can't be heard

## lost boy

what is this void
i'm trying so hard to fill?
what was once there
and where did it go?

i've been desperately searching
for answers
to all the questions i've ever asked myself

i try so hard
to regulate my fear of the unknown
i end up losing control
of the things i've kept

i think i'll spend the rest of my life
looking for something
i'll never be able to find

## cancer

it happened
more than once
i was defeated
in the battle to keep myself alive

and it'd cross my mind
if i'd die from cancer
they'd speak of me
and say

he fought so hard

yet on the other hand
if i'd die from suicide
they'd say
no fight was had

he gave up

## boulders to the beach

i left you behind
because i didn't believe i could stay with you
and survive

for too long
i'd been blowing crystals from my lungs
and aiming it at the stars
i'd fall asleep
to dream of the times i was happy
and open my eyes
to a nightmare of dusty floors and dead ends

home
is the only place i'd ever wanted to be
and every single time i tried
i never made the cut
a heavy metal door would slam itself shut
and i had no choice but to leave you behind

i packed my bags
no wine or vodka or bacardi
and i prepared to say goodbye
but i needed to see you
one last time
in all your shattered impermanent glory

i drove your broken bottle streets
i remembered the blurry nights on your corners
the kicks in the teeth
the soaking wet shoes
the ripped-up shirts
and the bleeding gums

a daily ceremony
of watching golden sunrises
with friends i'd made
and never given names

# edgewater

in the early morning mist
when the sun had barely broken
through the trees
i walked along
i walked alone

the obscure icy lake
turned my breath to frost
as it left my lips

and suddenly

i felt it

the world around me paused
the birds hushed their songs
the wind stopped blowing
and in the silence
i heard you –

you'll be alright

the sun // had barely broken // edgewater lake AUSTRALIA

acrylic

if there's a sign on the road

that tells me where to go

it does nothing

to change

where the road will lead me

the road had no signs // i still moved // maribyrnong AUSTRALIA

## almond latte

my grandmother showed me
a world of strength
through her eyes
where all things were good
right and sincere
she taught me fortitude
mostly – she taught me love

and then
i said goodbye to her
as if we were two people
who'd met in a cafe
shared a lifetime of stories
and left
wanting more
but knowing some day
we'd meet there again

almond lattes // come and go // wantirna AUSTRALIA

## sonata

she is
the first place i called my home
the truest feeling of safety i ever knew

she is
the first language i ever came to speak
the softest soil my feet stood upon

she is
the homeland from where i descend
the landscape
its flora and fauna

she is
my national anthem

she is
my mother

## renaissance // for her

the day you died
was the day i learned to grieve
it became
the end of all i had come to know about life

i keep getting up
perhaps
a little slower than before

still
i get up

the greatest

fate
was responsible
for the first strong knots
which found me
tied me to her
but the bonds
which grew
from the time
in a young boy's life
when we shared
our spirits and hearts
are so much harder to break
than anything
formed by blood

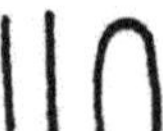

# the pugilist

MY ENTIRE WANT FOR GOODNESS
IS BORN FROM MY DESIRE
TO BE HAPPY

## call to arms

i'm ready and waiting
i'm prepared
to do something difficult
probably
the hardest thing i'll ever do

along the way
i'll figure out who i am
it won't be easy to stay strong
but i'll discover what i'm truly made of

and this will be
the greatest thing i'll ever achieve

## midnight decisions

i've scoured through so many men
          coffees and dinners
          one night stands and temporary boyfriends
hoping to find someone who'll protect me
save me from the bad things
to tell me
despite the hideous things i've endured
i'll be okay

then i realised – i'm tired
          of being used
          of being judged
          of wanting more from myself

i've always been worthy
but somewhere along the line
someone decided i wasn't
and i believed him

## mirror talk

i know it hurts
i know you can't stand it
but one day
you'll look back on this grief
as a collection of beautiful moments

your face will lift
your feet will balance

you'll walk
from the darkness of your room
into the ultraviolet light
of the world outside

it'll be written
in the earth beneath you
you were mourning
but you weren't slipping

your heart was broken
your life was changing

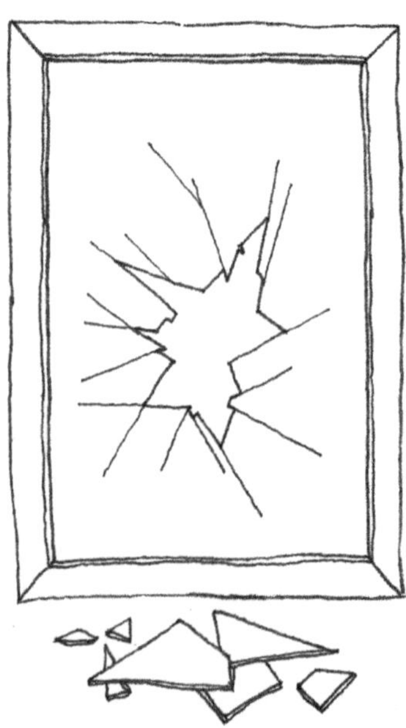

## carpe noctem

stay calm and composed
and call to your strength
to brave the storm

stay certain and steady
and let the chaos that surrounds you
be o//r//d//e//r//e//d

don't allow anything or anyone
take your energy away from you

you are
brave
strong

you are
enough

# better

i want you to know
i'm okay
          with this
          with seeing you

i love you still
i always will
but it'll only live
tucked away
in a small form
in a crevice of my heart

it'll always be there
always real
always

i'd never liked the way i looked
the colour of my skin
my scars and lines
the shape of my legs and hips
my wiry hair

someone did love it all
and he saw through it
he knew the soul
living in this frame
he heard the heart
beating in this chest
he helped me to see
my divine uniqueness

i don't think
he's the only one who sees me
there are others like him
chasing a meaning
depth and connection
instead of physical interactions
with impending expiry dates

when i think of this
i realise
there's nothing to be afraid of
i should step confidently
through this world
or i'll never know
how beautiful it is
when bent flowers bloom

## un bel di

one day
i'll take my turn
and leave my home
whether it be my city
or my country
and i'll run after my greatest dreams

i'll leave behind friends
and lovers too
so many what-ifs
to search the world for intricate purpose

i'll defy my fear
of things i don't know
i'll point my face to solar flares
and think of all the things
i've never done before
and without reasoning
i'll do it all

it'll be
in the fear and the uncomfortable
in the leaving
i'll find adventure and freedom
and when i find me
i'll find love

## blank page

you might not write about me
but that's alright

i write not for
nor about you
but for me

and my own legacy

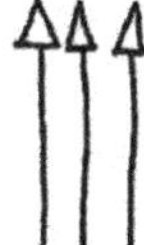

## bewildered at six and seven

sky gazing in the frozen night
trying to grasp the depth of what i'm looking at
the path which brought me here – lit by the moon
        three hundred and eighty-four thousand
        four hundred kilometres away

incomprehensible!

the mechanism making my body tick
planted only centimetres inside my chest
replacement parts available if need be
but no hope for the needy

maybe i'm a little stupid
and maybe i think like a child
because in my head
is a list of shit i can't understand
and i wonder if i'm chasing a dream
or just attempting greed

## driftwood

i'd left the small-town life behind
with no intention of ever returning to it
not because i didn't like it
but because
i always knew i'd leave

it was part of my life's great romance
the idea of being a creature
destined for adventure
and as far as i could imagine
it lay in the cold concrete of melbourne
not in the dry grass of the kimberley

there were days i'd feel at home
or at least
pretend i knew what it was
i'd be sitting somewhere – perhaps doing something
and it'd feel right
and i'd think

    i wish this could last forever

of course
nothing can stay
and i had to leave my home
to maybe come back one day
and love it again
for previously unknown reasons

the risk i took was
in the move toward unseen horizons
i could lose what i had then
and not find anything at all

## moonlit magnolias and madness

nothing can be said
that hasn't already been heard
oceans of raw emotion
portrayed and expressed
then undressed
and displayed
through different torrential variations
and depths of words

i wander this world
in a state of disarray
no destination
no eye on any prize
no known future beyond the now
it's dysphoric and grave
yet still i stay in these cold complexities
with such old and deepening convexities
lessening me
until i'm no more

life through emerald windows
closed crimson doors
i hear the sand
slipping through by the hour
the pills and the powder
the dismal skies
the clouds forming brainstorms
that strike me down and grow louder
drowning my portrait
of omnipotent beauty and power

take a breath
when you open your eyes
i'll still be here
only if you truly left
to traverse the seas
of the world's suffering
we could shed these shells of flesh
as autumn crosses us
yet you sit on your own
waiting
for the reaper to collect your soul
anticipating
languishing and suffering
all alone

there's something in these bones
jagged – jarred – and loose
what's the use in resisting?
i'm ragged and scarred and recluse
too bruised to go on existing
my crooked soul
in a constant state of shifting
but moonlit magnolias appear above me in the sky
i see them
from the corners of my tired eyes
as a great blue brightness
lights and ignites the parts of me
that i keep and hold
locked away
deep inside

## pas de regrets

i never regret anything that's happened to me
whether it be
making a bad choice
saying the wrong thing
doing something i shouldn't have done
not doing something i should have

no matter where i end up
i'll be
exactly where i'm meant to be

i underwrite each of my choices
i learn
and grow
with every decision i make

i'm always going to say how i feel
i'm going to be me
and i'm going to be okay with that

and that's one thing
i definitely will not regret

## idol

i'm one
a celestial being
a designer
an architect

i'm more than a man
i am the alpha
the omega
and everything that lies in between

here
within me
exists an eternal wisdom
the birth force of the universe
the sacred light of infinite energy

all that was
all that is
all that ever will be

## blood tree in the field

a mother
with eyes holding a delicate sadness
from what she's seen

a brother
whose shoulders are broad
so he can carry the world

an olive-skinned sister
who can't seem to see herself
through green eyes

another
who hides freckles on her face
with tufts of blonde hair

a father
whose voice is quiet and raspy
from years spent screaming

forlorn children
of predetermined purpose
born of innocent uniqueness

a twinkle and a shimmer
carrying me from infancy
into my older years

harsh lessons and taunts
pushed me
toward a life of insecurity

walking the same strides
of strong maternal legs
generations before me

reaching through darkness
to find freedom
from the past

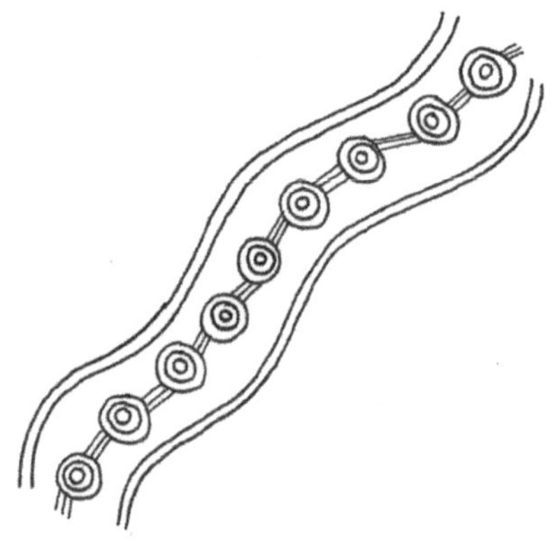

the hopeful longing
of all the things
i ever wanted

adventure in nature
fingers dancing on ivory
and songs sung loudly

never forgetting
the heartbreaking challenges
of a misguidedly good brotherhood

a fight for myself
to never forget who i am
where i'm from

the origins of my patrimony
casting me from a mould
and gifting me the same blood

the imaginative child
who never wanted to come inside
because he was afraid

they're each and all
the glance
and the thought

the feeling of belonging
that you can only know
from home

the constant reminder
as much as i am them
they are me

## liyarn ngarn

i'll kiss my family goodbye
i'll put distance between us
time after time

but i'll carry them with me
within my heart
my mind
and my stomach

i don't live in this world alone
because they are the world
which lives deep within me

## ode

to a man i loved
strong and deep
i thank him
for choosing to leave me for someone else

i wasn't solid enough
to leave him then
but i'm stronger now
than i've ever been before

and i'll never look behind me
to where he is
to where he'll stay

## draw your swords

i think i was nine
when a stranger first asked me if i liked boys
it was a regularly hot day
i could see the trees sway as the dust flew my way
i looked back at him
the one who judged me before knowing my name
the one who saw a boy in chains
yet never opened his mouth again

i'd never heard this question before
at a time when my best friends were boys
my bmx bike filling an empty void
with the bush as my home
the hills as my toys

i think i was fifteen
when i first lost hope of being happy
it was a regularly hot eve
and i could see the sweat
edge its way through my sleeve
as i grieved for notions – preconceived
by the uneducated or ill-informed

it was then i learned of the meaning
of gay and straight
and the differences between
how gay boys have glitter stashed in their pockets
and photos of other boys
hidden in their secret gold lockets

i think i was sixteen
when i first regretted who i was
it was a regularly hot night
and i could feel the stillness of my face
match the stillness of the light
i hadn't grown up conventionally
and didn't want my sexuality known
by women who lived by the script
and men who made pubs their home

but if by walking around
and carrying boulders
of lies on my shoulders
impaired my own opinion of me
how could i continue
living so fearfully?

i was eighteen
when i finally forgave myself
it wasn't my fault
i liked who i did
i shielded myself from the nay-sayers
trying to keep my heart hidden beneath layers
just like i did
my hopes and dreams

it's not their fault
they believe in quickly created lies
by others who despise
people like me
kindness and honesty are my answers
and i forgave myself
before i did so anyone else

i was eighteen
when the heat subsided
i stood with my head held high
and i danced with my heart showing
for all to see

i'm not ashamed of who i am
because lies and whispers and stories
don't define one single thing
about me

## grateful nectar

you fell down

you stood back up

you pushed through

you gave me values

you made me strong

you survived

## more than these bones

no need
to forever be searching for something or someone
to hold onto tightly with both of my hands
a life full of seemingly wrong choices made
apparently wrong paths walked
and supposed time wasted
looking and trying and searching
while defining – and finding – myself

discovering a path of possibility
which never seemed to have an end
two feet
constantly gripping soft dirt
to find their place on the earth
hoping
to build the trust in myself
to prove i have what it takes
to be myself
and to accept who i truly am
without hesitation or justification
to always stand tall with an upright back
for everything i believe in
no need
to ever walk in someone else's faded footsteps
no need
to ever manipulate my gait
to fit the stride of someone who went before me
to push on and on
in the wilderness of the rest of my thirties
and forge my own path

always listening
to the uneven beat of my heart
feeling the blood
feeding the creases of my fingers and toes
connecting my magnetic mind
to every single cell
as they race each other through my veins

searching for traces of spirit
to paint the portrait of my genesis
to listen
to each and every word i feel the need to speak
to find freedom and liberty
from the ropes and chains i bound to myself as a child
to live in a world
where a dream is born on a summer pillow
and it shows me
happiness was never about you
        always about me

looking up
at the endless cotton sheet sky
and searching for silhouettes of birds
following them in foolish dance steps
from here – to wherever they go
staying on course
with courage
mustered from the pit of my stomach
running toward the whereabouts of my vista
one day meeting the sun

staring deeply into my own soul
from the windows of my blinders
to a depth where my body collapses inward
so i find myself at the very beginning
the birth of this galaxy
and the universe which safely cradles it
seeing things for what they truly are
in boldness and grace
not what i once perceived them to be

knowing
i'm more than what they say i am
i'm more than this body
i'm more than this skin
more than these bones

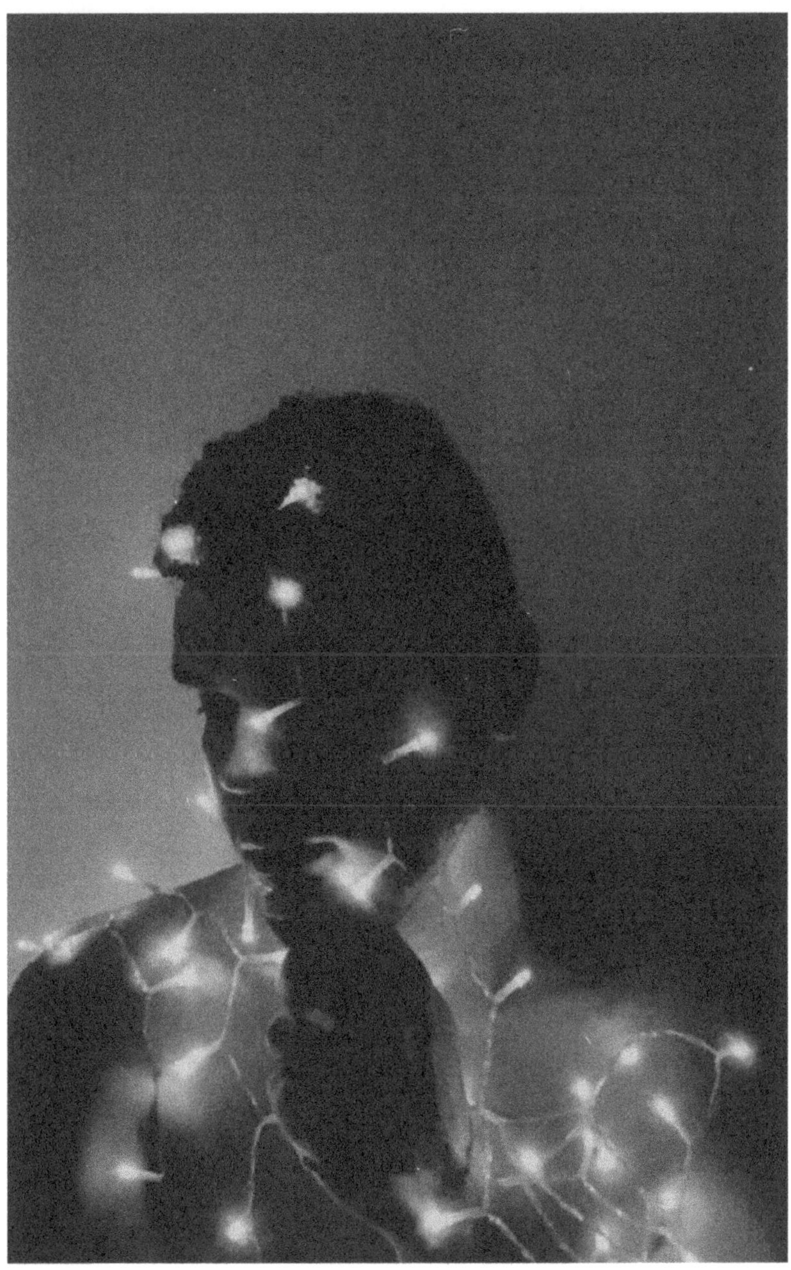

photograph me // capture more than these bones // melbourne AUSTRALIA

you may never learn the language you wanted to
you might never take the trip you'd dreamt of
the things that excited you when you were young
won't bring you the same joy they once did

you have to remember
to be brave enough to live anyway
write the rules you want to follow
and if the choice you made
was to break these rules
in the hunt for freedom
never apologise

promise me – promise yourself
you'll build your kingdom
you'll never look before you step
you'll be whoever you wish to be
as long as it's who you truly are

## nocturne

i've sat through so many nights
and i can't believe it's taken me this long
and all these moons
to realise there are so many stars
that shine in the dark

## philodendron

i took a leaf from the philodendron which grew in the glass vase
on the dining room table
the short snap sound of the stem ended the green life it had

in a couple of days
it'll be yellow and then turn brown

it won't matter
i'll have tossed it into the garden by then
and it will start sharing its residue with the undergrowth
feeding a commune of roots and insects

proof
when one bond breaks
another life begins

life // is a philodendron // nothing gold can stay // melbourne AUSTRALIA

## the pugilist

i want my eyes
to be always looking at the horizon
i don't ever want them to look away
so i won't lose sight of where i'm going
not knowing
wherever it was
i started

i'll stop myself
from looking too far up
because the sky doesn't hold my answers

anything i might ever seek
to aid the answering
of any question i might have
lies here
within me
and in the hearts of the people i love

i'll never question my whereabouts
at any point in time
i know
i'll always be treading where my dreams are meant to be
in the constellation of aries
between two spaces
of blue and white

if i never feel love
i know it's alive inside of me
and there's an entire life in knowing
anything i might never see
will always be here
because just like the sun
i'll surely be

## eucalyptus

i'm made up of pieces
of all the things i remember

i'll be
what i loved most
about the things that are gone

and i know
what i lose
will come around again
in another form

## clear the table [sms]

how can i allow myself time to grieve, when i have a life to live? a job to be worked and bills to pay?

it's in the moments i'm alone, when it comes creeping up on me. the unmissable feeling of needing her. so much so, i can barely bring myself to walk.

i've learned that the right thing to do, to handle grief during seeming normality, is to make room. and allow it to completely consume me.

the waves of sadness will never stop coming. i've accepted this and i'm okay with it.

because in the desperation and neediness, when i feel hopeless and lost, i know i was loved deeply by her. and i loved her totally.

everything i gave her was so kindly returned to me.

the table is cleared.

and i'm saving her a seat. my grief will stay with me, but it'll always be welcome.

I FELT PERPLEXED
SENT MY FRIEND A TEXT
DON'T KNOW WHAT'S NEXT

## nyalkardi

a beginning to this world and this chaotic life

spirit ancestors spinning silk
made from the dust of the milky way
plucking stars and comets from the heavenly ether
and crushing them by hand
into small pieces of light

the creation of vastness of sky
and endless stretching of land
and into it
carving the oceans
and the rivers
and the lakes

a universal life was given to a notion of time and place
with a purpose
to protect for the goodness of new

my people
were born from this land – littered with celestial particles
and when we die
it's where we'll return
for perpetual demonstration

to walk silently shoeless
on sunburned dirt or water-soaked grass
is to unite with the creators
through the pores on the soles of my feet
two portals
to freely move
from the soil and the grass leaves
into my born-black spirit
to calibrate my liyarn
for life navigation

my wondrous inheritance from my ancestor king
born with the name nyamwa
to protect me across forms and dimensions

i received my greatness
beginning with the energy of the universe
into the light
which moves
from the tops of the trees
into the roots of the earth

white skin
dotted with freckles and loose strands of blonde hair
a heart that bleeds black blood
and beats to the sound of a warrior's drum

NYALKARDI // MY SKIN NAME

i'm the ochre // the hand // which paints the cave // abbotsford AUSTRALIA

## chaplin

you can speak

and tell me

what rests on your mind

but if you mute your words

and talk to me instead

with the voice of your actions

you reveal to me

what can be found

inside your heart

# minuet

though this universe

i hold as my own

i possess not a single thing

for i can't know

the as yet unknown

if to the known

i always cling

## swan song

there's a sound in my head
and i think of it
as a bird

i can't recall
which sings this way
but
if i lay still

maybe
it'll teach me new songs
perhaps
one with less grit
and a melodic breathing method

something less hectic
than the steps i'm taking
to lightly rediscover
the legacy i'm making

crescendo

somewhere
on some distant planet
at some time
and by some how
the life you live
will reflect the very thoughts you think now

this belief
is unchanging
no amount of violence can atone
the structure you're currently building
is the one
you'll live in alone

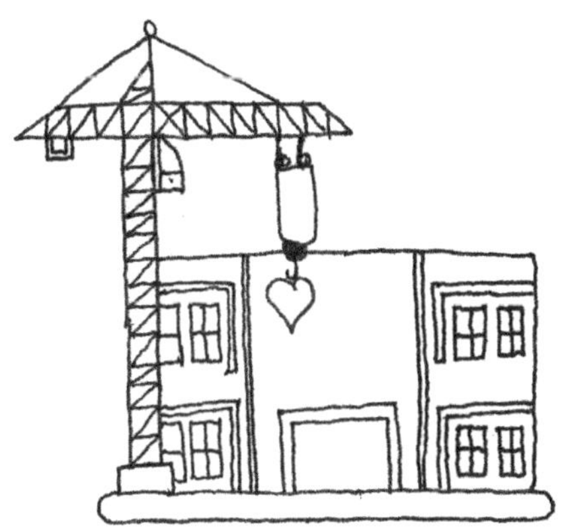

LOVE IS HOW YOU ACT TOWARD SOMEONE
NOT HOW YOU FEEL ABOUT THEM

## eclipse

the wandering
and not the waiting

the magic of lost feet
stumbling down a gravel road

the way the moon
never hangs the same

what if it's there

and not here

i'm meant to be?

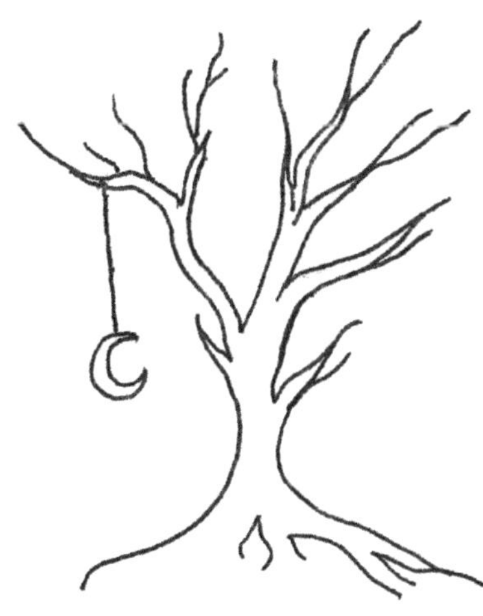

## blood moon

like the moon
we're allowed to eclipse too

and when we do
everything is okay
because the eclipse will never become darkness

the light always returns

it's the same
as the survival of the soul

within my heart
there's been
an uncomfortable and painful feeling
as if something was once there
and now it's missing
but when i think
of every magical moment
we shared together –

i'm released

you turned around
and walked away
but how blessed
am i to know
i'll have you
wherever i go?

so – go!
live the rest of your life
spread your beauty
around this giant planet of ours
but promise to take care of yourself

i'll see you again
if not in this life
then in the next

mind

body

soul

## versailles

i find myself
wishing for what i think is right
but how can i know the secrets of life?
if i keep clinging to what i know
then i'll miss so much of it

the one thing i see now is
holding onto control
only drains me of life
and turns it into an endless fight

what if i stopped for a moment – one sliver of time
and put what i'm holding
on hold?

maybe then
i'll see there's no need
to look at the world
through a stained-glass window
there's no need
to cover my eyes
from the way things are

i could then see how
i've been keeping myself out of the light
how i've been holding on
to the lonely gold of what i think is right for me
when really
there's no way for me to know
the span of the universe

how can i know the depth of my existence
when i've broken it up into pieces
hoping to be the maker?
i can't choke life into being what i want it to be

i'm not the designer of what i see
but i am in charge of how it's seen
so
i don't renounce the world
or how i see it

if i look from a place within
then i can clearly see
how i see what i see
is all i need to control

and letting go
of the ties which pull me away from peace
allows me to hear
the still space inside of me
and i see
the truth for what it is
not what i wanted it to be

things can be different
but i'm not alone
in my quest to see another way
if i release my struggle
then i can stop grasping for the answer
and i can stop wishing
for 'someday'

there's a greater plan
and a higher intelligence
and to it
i say:

help me let go of wishing

so my heart
may match the heartbeat
of a better way

plant my feet firmly in the soil of today

reset my sight
so from this moment
i feel no need to stray

there's a call to let go
of what's not meant for me to hold

acceptance is what i want right now
this is life's true gold

every single moment of surrender
is a peace treaty with my soul

searching// from my window // for gold // my soul // versailles FRANCE

# stardust

when it's hard to see clear
there are still chances to believe
in these pockets of no fear
there's a little space to breathe

i take moments as i please
and trust the light will take me far
i know i can always go with ease
because i was born from the stars

# common galaxia

each day
is born with a sunrise
and ends in a sunset
the same way
i open my eyes to see the light
and then close them
to hear the dark

i have no control
over how my story
begins or ends
but by now
i should know
all things have an ending

every spark
returns to darkness
every sound
returns to silence
every flower
returns to sleep in the earth

the journey of the sun
the journey of the moon
they're predictable

but mine is made of stardust
and it rides on the tail
of a silver comet

emancipation

i'm letting it go
▪
▪
▪
▪
▪
▪
letting it all go
▪
▪
▪
▪
▪
▪
to make room
▪
▪
▪
▪
▪
▪
for everything
▪
▪
▪
▪
▪
▪
that's waiting
▪
▪
▪
▪
▪
▪
to be let in

become a balloon // let it all go // fly away // edgewater AUSTRALIA

to you

to love
and be loved
to never forget your own insignificance

to never get used to the violence
the vulgar disparity of life around you

to seek joy
in the saddest of places
to pursue beauty to its cave

to never simplify what's complicated
or complicate what's simple

to respect strength
never power

above all –

to watch
to try and understand
to never look away

and to never – never –
forget

[should i find myself reflecting]

love
and be loved
never forget your own insignificance

never get used to the violence
the vulgar disparity of life around you

seek joy
in the saddest of places
pursue beauty to its cave

never simplify what's complicated
or complicate what's simple

respect strength
never power

above all –

watch
try and understand
never look away

and never – never –
forget

[should i find myself]

# brighton

i can sit
on the edge of the world

but take away the solid surface
of the earth beneath me
and i find myself

dreaming

my eyes wide open

failing to fulfil
any of my hopes

boardwalk // bayside // beneath the blue // brighton AUSTRALIA

## internally eden

there's a universe inside me
an ocean
with a constant changing tide
and snow-covered mountains
with tops which touch the sky

white and black birds
migrating north
a dusty desert wind
and wild rivers
carving out my name

i see
in explosions of sunlight
i feel
in the night
when it rains

the world within me
is greater than anything
i've ever known by far

i am the universe in motion
and i was born from the stars

## albatross

this life
is a migration of growth

without experience
of pain and discomfort

i'd simply be
a very different human

most definitely
a much lesser one

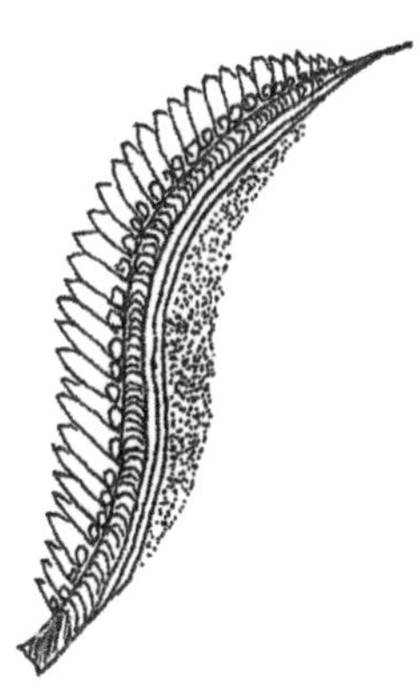

## skyline

staring deeply
into those bright city lights
i know you're beneath them
somewhere
dancing through streets of trams and cars
exploring laneways
of graffiti and dumpsters

maybe you're looking up
at the blue beams of the rialto
stretching your focus
in search of stars
all you seem to find
is the blurry glow
of auburn and gold
and cherry pollution

maybe you're wondering
if someone you passed
with or without locking a gaze
was the one
who'd one day
hold your heart
without ever letting go

you're out there
somewhere
beneath the city lights i see
spinning around lampposts
in smoky air
as i'm beneath the stars
you try to find

look beyond what you can already see
go further
than where you've already been
and we can do together
the things
you've always dreamed

sitting // on the roof // of the world // skyline // melbourne AUSTRALIA

## flannelette sheets

the time i like most

is four a.m.

when your heart beats

slow and deep

which i'm yet to discover

because i'm under the covers

still

and fast asleep

## paradigm

can i truly be patient?

not in my ability to wait
but to be calm
no matter what might happen

to take action
and always turn a moment
into a movement of growth

to have faith
and believe
everything will work out in the end

while i wait for the answer
i find myself
patient

## midday on new street

you're a volcano at touch
an earthquake at heart
you're a hurricane in mind
a forest in entirety

you lay full of secrets
hiding and waiting
you're a mystery
but one i trust

you dream in technicolour
and speak in golden hues
you fight
with fire and bone
for the nature of your name

for you
life is art
but the way you live
is beyond any masterpiece
i've ever seen

your long smile
how it shrinks your eyes
it gently catches
your strength and softness
the human nature i see
when i look at you

it's hard to believe –
in your words
there's a delicate promise

it makes me want to give up
everything i thought i knew
about what it means
to be good

you make me fly // thru elsternwick park // to you // brighton AUSTRALIA

## plain sailing // skyline pt ii

i'd look into the city lights
so many times
knowing
he was in there somewhere
dancing down a cobblestone alleyway
exploring the greatness of his life
always patient and steady
with one foot in front of the other

he'd be the nicest compliment
i'd ever receive
spoken from kindness and grace
by the voice of the universe
in the silence of night

he'd be my one
and our bodies would fit together
like a puzzle
but he wouldn't puzzle me

he'd understand me
and he'd challenge me
he'd tell me when i'm wrong
and when i'm right
and he'd always speak to me with
thoughtful sincerity
never callousness
never harm

he'd be my one
our hands would press together
like pieces of paper
but they wouldn't be blank

they'd be scribbled with words like –

BE KIND.
GRATITUDE IS THE GREATEST GIFT.
I ENCOURAGE YOU TO BE THE BEST YOU CAN.
<u>ALWAYS</u> <u>LOVE</u>.

i'd learn from him // he'd learn from me
i'd inspire him // he'd inspire me

i'd trust him
my heart
would find a home in his
i'd continue to grow
into the greatest being i can be

yet
i'd always remember
nothing in life is permanent
my adventure is temporary
love is the only thing that matters
cos it's the only thing
we leave behind

i'd look into the city lights
so many times
knowing
he was in there somewhere
exploring the greatness of his life
always patient and steady
with one foot in front of the other

perhaps not down a cobblestone alleyway
but maybe
in a black buttoned shirt
with big brown eyes
and salt speckled hair
in a corner cafe
on ormond road

## little white dove

when a sadness falls
on the morning bird
you tend to wonder
what the day will bring

but you close your eyes
and lift your head
because at least
the bird still sings

## dear dov

you're a beautiful flower
you aren't afraid to bloom
you can grow even taller
you have so much more room

a storm can come and catch you
the wind can toss you around
but you'll still stand strong
cos you grow in such solid ground

i know your heart will beat better
your mind will feel right
your liyarn will reconnect
your chest won't feel so tight

although hearts and souls
are unpredictable like the weather
i know you'll be okay
and by okay – i mean – greater than ever

dov // boee // mi'ma'amakim // greater than ever // melbourne AUSTRALIA

## endless winter afternoon

there's no questioning
you entered my life
at the exact point of my need

maybe it was a coincidence
or

whatever it was
i can be certain
you came to make me smile

and on a good day
to make me feel

SOMETIMES THE SIMPLEST SOLUTION
OUT OF BROKEN LOVE
IS BECOMING HIS FRIEND
INSTEAD OF SAYING GOODBYE

clear sky // no questions // endless winter afternoon // geelong AUSTRALIA

## lambada

wherever you go in life
don't forget who you are
the strong man you were
before we both met
everything that still lives
deep in your wildflower heart

remember when you told me
i touched you with warmth and assurance
and i watched you intently
with kind brown eyes
i was the one who listened
to the transcription of your soul
in real time

i first felt your spirit
when i traced my fingers across your back

i first saw your power
when i looked at you on glen huntly road

i first heard your glory
when you spoke of your pain

know –
you've changed my life
by touching my heart
and one day
when you find yourself by the beach
dancing the lambada again
you'll remember –
you can never be darkened
because you were born from the light

to hear sounds
which haven't been heard
to see colours and shapes
not yet known
to try to understand
the subtle power
found in every part of the earth

to fly
and find pure ethereal substances
not made of matter
but instead
an invisible soul-penetrating reality

to hear another heart
and softly
whisper something back to it

to be
a light in the dark
an umbrella in the rain

to feel
much more than to know

to be
the eyes of a bird
the top of a mountain
the edge of a cliff

to be the ocean
and understand the moon
despite its changes

to be a tree
and read the memories of leaves
with every season

to be an insignificant human
standing on a street in a giant city
watching
waiting
wondering

to be the smile on someone's face
a moment they saved without planning
to shine in their eyes
when they think of a place
when they think of a time

to be remembered

as love

turn sadness // into something beautiful // wilsons promontory AUSTRALIA

## About Bebe Backhouse

Hailing from the Kimberley region of north-Western Australia, Bebe Backhouse is a descendant of the Bardi Jawi people, who has called Narrm (Melbourne) home for ten years. Beginning his creative practice as a classical pianist and composer, Bebe was awarded a West Australian Youth Award at age 21 for his work as a music teacher to young Indigenous people. He later made a name for himself as a creative producer and director of youth theatre, festivals, and public art projects across Australia, including international dance and theatre projects in New Zealand, France and Belgium. While holding senior positions at leading public arts organisations in Melbourne, Bebe successfully fostered many artistic opportunities for Aboriginal and Torres Strait Islander creatives to showcase their work in mainstream platforms, allowing Traditional Culture to thrive in the public realm.

A leader in designing and delivering high-profile programs and strategic projects for Australia's diverse communities, Bebe is a frequent commentator on the arts and culture community. Holding cultural integrity at the forefront, he has a passion for advocacy, advancement, and the health and wellbeing of Aboriginal and Torres Strait Islander people.

After being published in the anthology *Growing Up Aboriginal in Australia*, edited by Anita Heiss, Bebe continues to share his life experiences through his writing, with the hope of enabling connection and inspiration.

*more than these bones* is Bebe's debut solo publication.